SANDINO IN THE STREETS

CARIBBEAN AND LATIN AMERICAN STUDIES
JACK W. HOPKINS, GENERAL EDITOR

SANDINO
IN THE STREETS

Photographs and Essay by Joel C. Sheesley

Translated and Edited by Wayne G. Bragg

Prologue by Ernesto Cardenal

Introduction by Jack W. Hopkins

INDIANA UNIVERSITY PRESS

Bloomington & Indianapolis

PRINTED IN HONG KONG

LIBRARY OF CONGRESS CATALOGING-IN-PUBLICATION DATA

SHEESLEY, JOEL C., DATE.
SANDINO IN THE STREETS / PHOTOGRAPHS AND ESSAY BY JOEL C. SHEESLEY ;
TRANSLATED AND EDITED BY WAYNE G. BRAGG ; PROLOGUE BY ERNESTO
CARDENAL ; INTRODUCTION BY JACK W. HOPKINS.
P.   CM. — (CARIBBEAN AND LATIN AMERICAN STUDIES)
INCLUDES TRANSLATED EXCERPTS FROM SANDINO'S "EL PENSAMIENTO VIVO,"
1981 ED.
INCLUDES BIBLIOGRAPHICAL REFERENCES.
ISBN 0-253-35207-X (CLOTH)
1. SANDINO, AUGUSTO CÉSAR, 1895–1934—PICTORIAL WORKS.
2. SANDINO, AUGUSTO CÉSAR, 1895–1934—QUOTATIONS.   3. NICARAGUA—
POLITICS AND GOVERNMENT—20TH CENTURY.   4. GRAFFITI—NICARAGUA—
PICTORIAL WORKS.   I. BRAGG, WAYNE G., DATE.   II. SANDINO,
AUGUSTO CÉSAR, 1895–1934. PENSAMIENTO VIVO. ENGLISH. SELECTIONS.
1991.   III. TITLE.   IV. SERIES.
F1526.3.S24S5   1991
972.8505'1'092—DC20   90-25231

1 2 3 4 5   95 94 93 92 91

C O N T E N T S

SANDINO IN THE STREETS

Translator's Preface

THE PURPOSE of this translation is to reveal, through his own writings, the thoughts and deeds of Augusto César Sandino, a key figure in Nicaraguan historical annals and contemporary Central American politics. Who was this man who inspires adulation and revolution, as well as a popular iconography unparalleled in Latin America? Liberators Bolivar and Martí are remembered mostly in museums and textbooks, while Sandino's image is in the public domain, seen everywhere in Nicaragua, and his ideas form the basis of an ongoing sociopolitical and economic revolution in Central America. Yet Sandino is largely unknown in the United States, the country that helped make him a hero to his own people.

To make Sandino's person and ideas accessible to the English-speaking world, we chose excerpts from the more than 600 pages of Spanish material available. This small book seeks to keep the meaning and impact of Sandino's thoughts and image by careful selection, condensation, and simplification. He was a prolific and careful writer, as he was a speaker. Reporter

Carlton Beals of *The Nation* went into the Segovian mountains in 1928 to interview this enigmatic (for the U.S.) figure, describing thus his conversations:

> His utterance is remarkably fluid, precise, evenly modulated; his enunciation is absolutely clear, his voice rarely changes pitch, even when he is visibly intent upon the subject matter. Not once during the four and a half hours, during which he talked almost continuously without prompting from me, did he fumble for the form of expression or indicate any hesitancy regarding the themes he intended to discuss. His ideas are precisely, epigrammatically ordered.[1]

Sandino used clear, colloquial, ornate, Nicaraguan Spanish, so my challenge was to make him understandable in contemporary American English without losing the flow and flavor of his ever-evolving thought. He wrote throughout his life and struggle—as a worker abroad, in the din of battle, as a husband and son, and as a national hero. The selections include letters, declarations, communiques, interviews, and autobiographical notes. Whole documents were rarely translated for lack of space. Repetitive and extraneous phrases and paragraphs were simply left out in the condensation process. I indicated ellipses sparingly, only where there was a gap in thought or events.

Sandino's sense of history and his desire to make his cause known to the world led him to document it carefully, making triplicates of everything, keeping all correspondence, and storing documents in different places as his army moved. He took a set to Mexico and left them in the Masonic Lodge in Mérida. He gave many documents to journalist Gustavo Alemán Bolaños that served as a basis for his book *Sandino, el libertador,* and also for Gregorio Selser's *Sandino, general de hombres libres* and *El pequeño ejército loco.* When the Nicaraguan National Guard seized Wiwilí after Sandino was assassinated, they found stores of files, which Anastasio Somoza García pirated to write an apocryphal book on Sandino. Even so, many documents have been lost, including those in Mérida. Many were maliciously destroyed by the Somocistas.

My source was the two-volume edition *Augusto C. Sandino: El pensamiento vivo,* edited, with introduction and notes, by Sergio Ramírez in 1981.[2] He added thirty-nine documents to the original edition done by Editorial Universitária Centroamericana, San José, Costa Rica (1974 and seven reprints). Volume II contains a chronology of events from 1890 to 1934, which was the basis for the historical timeline in our book.

The references in brackets given at the end of each entry in our book refer to the sources of original documents used by Ramírez, and found in Documentary Sources at the end of this book. The second set of references indicate the volume and page(s) of the citation from *Augusto C. Sandino: El pensamiento vivo* by Ramírez.

Sandino's life and ideals shaped the thinking of the *muchachos* who kept his vision alive and sparked the insurrection that triumphed in 1979. In 1961 Carlos Fonseca, the leader of the Sandinista popular revolution, wrote *Viva Sandino,* a political interpretation of some of Sandino's writings. Like Fonseca, most of the young leaders of the Sandinista revolution died for the cause, as Sandino himself did. But *sandinismo* triumphed, because, as the preface to the first Costa Rican edition of our source noted:

> Each of the ideas expressed by Sandino is in some measure backed by his struggle; there is a direct correlation between his thought and his action. Nothing is said gratuitously here and it is this vital and visceral correlation that strips his language of all rhetorical contamination, a beautiful

language, as is every expression of the truth. [I: 22]

Sandino had a primary school formal education, but his inquisitive mind and moral convictions explain his eloquence. To fully appreciate his beautiful language and the impact of his thought, Sandino should be read in the original. All texts lose in translation.

Sandino is universal. Not only Central Americans but also people and nations everywhere who have felt the oppressor's boot will understand Sandino's insistence on human dignity, non-intervention, and sovereign self-determination. Sandino's human side is revealed in his letters to Blanca, his communiques to his generals, and his treatment of his men and family. His brilliant military strategy presaged guerrilla tactics of today. Sandino's political views of Latin American and Indian solidarity are still relevant in the face of the neo-colonial economic dependency and indebtedness of recently industrializing Latin America that adversely affect the masses. An isthmus canal across Nicaragua is still perceived as needed, since the Panama Canal is too narrow for most modern tankers and will soon be controlled by Panama.

Sandino Vive because the democratic and patriotic ideals he struggled for are unresolved—the struggle for national integrity, self-determination, and human dignity. I dedicate my labor of translation to these ideals that Sandino embodied and expressed so eloquently in word and deed, and to those who have paid the ultimate price for pursuing these ideals.

Wayne G. Bragg

N O T E S

1. Carlton Beals, "With Sandino in Nicaragua: Send the Bill to Mr. Coolidge," *The Nation,* Vol. 126, No. 3272 (March 21, 1928), pp. 314–316.

2. *Augusto C. Sandino: El pensamiento vivo,* con introducción, selección y notas de Sergio Ramírez. Managua: Editorial Nueva Nicaragua, 1981. Permission to translate from this two-volume edition has been granted by Editorial Nueva Nicaragua, Managua.

Prologue

ERNESTO CARDENAL

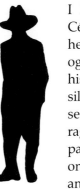 I BELIEVE that Augusto César Sandino is the only hero in history who is recognized by his people by his silhouette alone. The silhouette of Sandino is seen everywhere in Nicaragua—on walls, on ramparts, on fences, on curbs, on columns, on bridges, and even on electric and telephone posts.

Furthermore, Sandino is a unique historical case: an assassinated hero who fifty years later rises again incarnated in an entire people and defeats those who had assassinated him. And thus he continues to live.

"SANDINO LIVES"—this was painted on a wall which the Cuban poet Cintio Vitier called to my attention right after the triumph of the Revolution, and which I had not noticed before. It did not say *Viva Sandino*, as the revolutionary and Catholic poet Cintio Vitier pointed out to me, which would have been the more natural and usual phrase, but rather *Sandino Vive*, which gave a more profound meaning, that of an act of faith and a proclamation of resurrection. To be sure, afterwards I have seen this phrase many, many times on the walls of Nicaragua which I noticed for the first time with Cintio Vitier: "SANDINO LIVES, THE STRUGGLE CONTINUES." And it appears in many instances together with the silhouette of Sandino. At times it is not a silhouette of Sandino's entire body but rather just his hat, and not even his Stetson hat but only a simple design of three lines—a kind of figure eight on its side with a sort of triangle on top—the broad hat brim of Sandino.

This silhouette found everywhere inspired me to do a sculpture of Sandino which President Daniel Ortega, after the loss of the elections and before the transfer of government, ordered constructed in great proportions (54 feet tall), dominating all of Managua. As an amateur sculptor, I had for thirty years been thinking of the problem of how to create a stylized sculpture of Sandino. It was exactly thirty years ago, around 1960, that I was a novice in a Trappist monastery in the United States and I remember that in the novitiate I set about to draw sketches of a monument to Sandino. I found that I could stylize his figure very well seen from the front or behind, that is, his silhouette, but not the details of his face, his hat, or his arms seen from another angle without making it a realistic, unstylized figure, which I did not

want. Never did I imagine that one day I would leave that monastery into which I had gone with the intention of staying all my life and that many years later there would be a revolution in Nicaragua and that I would be commissioned to do a monument of Sandino. It was, as I said, while meditating on this silhouette which the people had created everywhere that the stylization that I sought occurred to me: a flat figure, nothing more detailed than a pure silhouette, which now towers above Managua. It was raised on the hill where Somoza's presidential palace once stood, thus becoming a symbol of the triumph of Sandino over Somoza and of the resurrection of Sandino after the death of *somocismo*.

Now we have this beautiful book which collects the images of Sandino in the streets, the Sandino of the people. Images of Sandino made by the people of Sandino, the ordinary people who created Sandino—accompanied by the words of Sandino, which, more than words, are the deeds of Sandino. Images, words, and deeds that are Sandino alive, resurrected.

Do not think that because the Frente Sandinista lost an election that Sandino and *sandinismo* have died in Nicaragua.

Rather, this loss by election has been the highest triumph of the Sandinistas. The Frente Sandinista had proposed to make a democratic revolution, with opposition parties and free elections. This has been fulfilled, and the elections were so free and honest that the Frente Sandinista lost. Democracy meant the possibility of losing this or any other election. Elections in which a party could never lose would not truly be free elections. They would be false elections in a false democracy and, for this reason, a false revolution. Nicaragua has also been the only case of a revolution which, having lost political power, does not lose as a revolution but rather goes on to become, democratically, an opposition party. Why were the elections lost? Because the military and economic pressures of the United States caused a very small percentage of the population who favored the Frente Sandinista to vote for another government not under attack by the United States. The election, in the final analysis, was between the Frente Sandinista and the government of the United States. By a small margin, and under much pressure, the United States won the election.

And the revolution which lost the election won, showing itself to be democratic.

And Sandino lives. If the new government removes the images of Sandino, it will remove them from the walls, the ramparts, and the electric posts, but not from the people. If a new *somocista* dictatorship is created, it will bring about a new insurrection and a new defeat of the new *somocismo*. Because Sandino lives.

As it is written on so many walls of Nicaragua:

"SANDINO LIVES AND THE STRUGGLE CONTINUES."

Managua, July 15, 1990.

(Translated by Wayne G. Bragg)

"SANDINO LIVES AND THE STRUGGLE CONTINUES."

Nicaragua: The Context of the Revolution

J A C K   W .   H O P K I N S

In his introductory essay, Joel Sheesley conveys very effectively the meaning of the images of Sandino in the street. His interpretation needs no addition from me, except to emphasize the importance of this street art, in his words, "as artistic expression, historical witness, political propaganda, national honor, even mythical longing." The images of Sandino collected and reproduced here are all those things, and they are more.

However, the deeper meaning of the image of Sandino can be appreciated more fully in the context of the political and social revolution that was inspired by his life as a determined nationalist rebel. My purpose here is to paint that context in broad strokes, not only as a means of linking the past with the present but also to empha-  size the vital importance and deep meaning of national sovereignty to the Nicaraguan people. Understanding Nicaraguan nationalism will help us understand also the powerful hold of Augusto César Sandino as an enduring hero of the Nicaraguan people. Much of the message of Sandino, part of which is reproduced here in his own words as a sidebar to the images of Sandino in the street, centers on the issue of Nicaraguan national sovereignty. The reader should absorb the images for their aesthetic impact, but they are greatly enhanced by the accompanying words of Sandino himself, as he recounts his struggles, his resistance to the foreign occupying force, his personal life during the years of guerrilla fighting, and his dreams for his country. The images are focused even more clearly by the historical timeline that highlights the events of the moment. Taken together, the photographic images, the words of Sandino, and the historical timeline comprise a powerful message.

The February 1990 elections in Nicaragua were only the most recent event in a long-unfolding process that seemed to reach its climax in the 1979 revolution. We must remember that much of the history of Nicaragua that shaped the revolutionary struggle of the 1970s and that propelled the long resistance of Sandino to the U.S. occupation of the 1920s and 1930s preceded *sandinismo* in the modern sense of that word. In many respects, what has been seen as a recent phenomenon in the form of the Frente Sandinista de Liberación Nacional (FSLN) is only a reiteration (with re-

finements to be sure) of earlier nationalist manifestations. One must delve further into Nicaraguan history to appreciate fully why the imagery of Sandino remains so viable and important in the Nicaragua of today, the February 1990 elections notwithstanding.

The roots of revolution in Nicaragua, as John Booth points out,[1] run deep in the country's history. The continuing factionalism of Nicaraguan society preceded its independence in 1832 and stemmed in part from features of the Spanish colonial system. Ideological disputes between Liberals and Conservatives—typical of much of post-independence Latin America—were exacerbated by conflicts arising from economic interests and the result has been a long history of violence and militarism. The geographical setting of Nicaragua has also complicated the country's development and made it vulnerable to all manner of foreign intervention during much of its history. A river and lake system (the Río San Juan and the Lago de Nicaragua) that offers a convenient and alluring route across the Central American isthmus has tempted outside powers to intervene, and this has led to sometimes violent internal political struggles. Finally, the country's dependence on certain key exports (princi-

pally coffee, beef, cotton, and sugar) has subjected it to the fickle fluctuations of world commodity markets and all the socioeconomic problems that such dependence causes. One result, with clear connections to the 1979 revolution, was class conflict, as the consequences of the dependent, export-oriented economy hit the lower socioeconomic classes most severely. An almost omnipresent element in Nicaragua's political history, from independence until the present day, has been the influence of outside forces. Their impact on Nicaraguan politics was magnified as domestic factions and individual politicians sought to gain advantage, one way or the other, from the foreign presence.

Sandino and *sandinismo* make more sense when seen in this historical context. Their powerful influence and their resonance among the Nicaraguan people reflect as much as anything the deep-rooted, long-continuing struggle to gain Nicaraguan mastery over Nicaragua.

Instances of outside intervention fill the history of the country. Although Nicaragua gained its independence from Spain essentially without violence, the country soon erupted into factional battles between Liberals and Conservatives. Weakened by that struggle, and foundering in a serious economic depression, Nicaragua became a tempting object for foreign powers interested in an interoceanic waterway. Domestic politics reflected the competition of different groups for external assistance in building a canal, all to no avail but also highly disruptive. Similarly, British commercial interests led to repeated intervention by Great Britain, including the seizure of Nicaraguan territory in 1847.

The situation was complicated further by the increasing interest of the United States in the Central American region, partly due to the search for an interoceanic route, which intensified as the California gold rush accelerated, but also a result of competition with the military and trade interests of Great Britain. For Nicaragua, the result was continuing crises, some stemming from the ripples of the Monroe Doctrine, some from the complex interaction of North American entrepreneurs, freebooters such as the infamous William Walker, and Nicaraguan politicians who sought to benefit from outside intervention.

The invasion of Nicaragua in 1855 by William Walker, an eccentric and fanatical soldier of fortune, following a dispute over the Accessory Transit Company (Cornelius Vanderbilt's shipping route across the isthmus),[2] stands as one of the landmarks in the struggle for Nicaraguan sovereignty. (Walker invaded Nicaragua at the invitation of the Liberals of León, who enlisted his aid against the Conservatives of Granada.[3] This illustrates well how so much of the foreign intervention in Nicaragua originated from Nicaraguan domestic struggles.) Walker captured the Conservative city of Granada, took command of the Nicaraguan army, and even had himself elected president. The battles against Walker's forces quickly became a struggle not only for Nicaraguan but also for Central American sovereignty. Walker's excesses, as he attempted to consolidate his power, served to rally resistance throughout Central America, until he finally surrendered and escaped to the United States in 1857. His end came in 1860 when, after several attempts to return to Nicaragua, he was captured by British forces and then executed by Hondurans.

The Walker intervention, however, is more than an interesting historical footnote, because such foreign intrusion into Nicaraguan affairs has been raised constantly as a rallying cry for revolution and national sovereignty. Walker thus became the *bête noire* as Sandino became the hero and the inspiration for the Revolution.

U.S. interest in direct intervention in Nicaragua diminished during most of the latter half of the nineteenth century as the United States became preoccupied with its own Civil War and continental expansion to the West. But that temporary U.S. disinterest in Nicaragua ended in 1909, when President Taft landed marines in Bluefields on the pretext of protecting U.S. lives and property after Liberal President José Santos Zelaya made the mistake of confiscating a U.S. mining concession, the La Luz and Los Angeles Mining Company. That intervention opened a quarter-century of chaotic politics in Nicaragua, and led to the rise of Augusto César Sandino.

Little would be served by a detailed account of the complex twists and turns of Nicaraguan politics during the twenty-five years that followed the U.S. intervention of 1909. The period has been described aptly by Sergio Ramírez (who was vice-president during the Sandinista government) as follows: "government among cousins and relatives who docilely continued turning the nation over to foreign interests, acquiring usurious debts, and giving more goods and resources as collateral."[4] The United States steadily became more deeply enmeshed in Nicaraguan affairs, occupying the country (except for short intervals) for the quarter-century after 1909. For all practical matters, the United States ran Nicaragua. As Hubert Herring describes it, "a supposedly sovereign republic had become the virtual ward of New York bankers, acting informally for the American government but without Senate authorization."[5]

Bad went to worse with the Bryan-Chamorro Treaty of 1914. Negotiated under suspicious conditions, the treaty "grants in perpetuity to the Government of the United States . . . the exclusive proprietary rights necessary and convenient for the construction, operation, and maintenance of an interoceanic canal." The price was $3 million, most of which went directly to the U.S. banks to which Nicaragua was indebted. The Bryan-Chamorro Treaty served only to heighten Nicaraguan resentment of the United States, which continually manipulated the country's affairs puppet-like.

The situation rapidly deteriorated, until, in 1926, the country's political affairs disintegrated into generalized conflict and eventually civil war. At the height of the conflict, the United States had committed eleven major warships and over five thousand marines. The action included U.S. bombing of the northwestern city of Chinandega (history records this attack as the first aerial bombing of a civilian population).[6] The civil war was ended by a cease-fire agreement—the Espino Negro Pact—signed at Tipitapa on 12 May 1927 by all the Liberal generals *except* Augusto César Sandino.

That holdout was to make all the difference. As Booth observes, Henry Stimson, who signed for the United States, "did not realize that he had in truth witnessed both the birth of a war of liberation and the conception of a revolution still a half century in the future."[7]

The images which Joel Sheesley has photographed represent a distillation of the profound influence of that stubborn and complex man Augusto César Sandino. Born in 1895 in Niquinohomo, a small town west of Granada, Sandino in his early years demonstrated no particular promise. Although his father, a dedicated Liberal, undoubtedly influenced the young man's political sympathies, Sandino's young manhood was undramatic. Working at a variety of jobs, he moved from Nicaragua to Honduras to Guatemala and finally to Mexico. The Mexican political environment, highly charged in the aftermath of the violent Mexican Revolution, helped shape his attitudes, his sympathy for the rural poor, and his resentment of foreign intervention in Central America and especially in his home country, Nicaragua. "But in the end," as Neill Macaulay observes, "it was Latin American nationalism that became Sandino's creed."[8]

Sandino returned to Nicaragua in 1926 and soon afterwards took on the task of organizing supporters to join and fight for the Liberals. His force eventually grew to some three hundred guerrillas. After Sandino, alone among the Liberal generals, refused to sign the Espino Negro pact, he moved to the northern mountains and continued the battle against the U.S. invasion force and the Guard. Despite the best efforts of the government forces and the U.S. Marines, Sandino survived and continued his struggle to 1933. Without doubt, Sandino was "one of the precursors of modern revolutionary guerrilla warfare."[9] The guerrilla war continued relentlessly from 1927 through 1933, attracting increasing support from the Nicaraguan people as the impact of U.S. intervention and the effects of the economic depression took hold. All the efforts of the U.S.-constructed National Guard and the U.S. Marines failed to stop Sandino's campaign.

The U.S. presence in Nicaragua had become frustrating and increasingly embarrassing as it became the object of satire and ridicule. Will Rogers asked, in 1929, "Why are we in Nicaragua, and what the Hell are we doing there?" Similar questions would be asked, and not just by comedians, for years to come. The mounting casualty toll aroused increasing opposition to U.S. intervention in Nicaragua; Congress, in 1932, eventually restricted funds for the military intervention. Finally, the United States reached the decision to pull out of Nicaragua after the 1932 elections.

Sandino, responding to critics who called him and his followers "common bandits," countered,

> Do you think that we could have existed half a year with all the might of the United States against us if we had been merely bandits? If we were bandits, every man's hand would be against us; every man would be a secret enemy. Instead, every home harbors a friend.[10]

Dana Munro of the U.S. State Department seemed to admit this when he wrote, "It is difficult to suppose that Sandino could have kept up the struggle, against great odds and in the face of severe hardship, if he had not been inspired by a fanatical hostility to foreign intervention."[11]

The U.S. role was filled quickly by the Nicaraguan National Guard, headed by Anastasio Somoza García, who rapidly became the most powerful force in Nicaragua. Sandino, who considered that his main task—to rid Nicaragua of foreign intruders—had been accomplished, quickly entered into negotiations with President Juan Sacasa to end the war, and agreed to a cease-fire on 2 February 1933.

Augusto César Sandino's life ended tragically on 21 February 1934, when, after dining with Sacasa in the presidential palace, he (as well as two rebel generals and Sandino's brother, Sócrates) was ambushed and murdered by National Guardsmen acting on the direct orders of Anastasio Somoza García. On the same night, the National Guard murdered some three hundred of Sandino's followers at his headquarters in Wiwilí.[12]

The murder of Sandino opened the way for forty-five years of tyranny in his country. Somoza quickly tightened his control of the National Guard, eliminating opposition in the top officer corps, and proceeded to force the resignation of President Sacasa. From that point, Somoza relentlessly extended his power base in the National Guard until he controlled essentially all public functions. The result was a dictatorial and thoroughly corrupt state, characterized by spying, terror, and all manner of brutal violations of human rights. Somoza García's corruption of the state apparatus and political institutions facilitated his conversion of the nation's economy into his own personal and family concession, so that the Somoza family, collaborators, and cronies reaped enormous riches from what should have been public resources. The key was, as Booth accurately concludes, that "virtually absolute political power is the most important economic resource one can possess."[13]

Though Anastasio Somoza García met a violent end in September 1956 at the hands of a printshop worker, Rigoberto López Pérez, that was not to be the end of the Somoza dynasty. Nicaragua suffered through twenty-three more years of corrupt and brutal rule by Luís and then Anastasio Somoza Debayle, the dictator's sons. The always somewhat tenuous grip of the Somozas on the country, a control that required careful and delicate balancing of the elements of power, began to erode in the late 1960s after Anastasio Somoza Debayle took over. Gradually both domestic and foreign opposition to the regime gained strength.

The Frente Sandinista de Liberación Nacional which grew out of student movements opposing Somoza in the 1940s and then began to organize as a guerrilla force in the early 1960s, suffered through some eighteen years of struggles, setbacks, and heavy casualties in repeated encounters with the National Guard. The final campaign turned into intense, widespread combat that involved thousands of people and that resulted in thousands of deaths before the Sandinista triumph in July 1979.

That Sandino lacked a fully developed ideology should in no way obscure the enormous and profound influence of the man and his life on the Sandinista revolution and on Nicaragua. The main elements of Sandino's ideas—resistance to U.S. and other foreign intervention, national sovereignty, populist social policies, agrarian reform—were incorporated into the ideology of the FSLN, amplified, and detailed. And this ideology, the core of *sandinismo*, served to vitalize the revolution and gave it moral strength as a small band of guerrillas steadily expanded into a victorious revolutionary force.

Americans often are perplexed by the reactions of other people to the foreign policies of the United States. But for Nicaraguans, as Macaulay reminds us, the wounds were deep:

> . . . a proud nation was humiliated, occupied militarily by insensitive and often bigoted foreigners, who left only after putting in place the elements for a sleazy native tyranny—a historical experience that many, perhaps most, Nicaraguans choose not to forget. Inspired by the example of the martyred Sandino, the latter-day Sandinistas remain determined to redeem the honor of their people by continued resistance to the United States. The hostility generated by this affair of more than half a century ago is a major factor in today's confrontation in Central America.[14]

The Nicaraguan elections of 25 February 1990, which the incumbent government headed by the Frente Sandinista de Liberación Nacional lost to the Unión Nacional Opositora (UNO), emphasize continuity rather than signifying the end of an ideology. That the Sandinistas lost the presidency, control of the National Assembly, and the majority of local municipal councils to the UNO coalition should not be interpreted to be the death of *sandinismo* any more than the murder of Augusto César Sandino in 1934 ended the influence of the man as hero, historical witness, and inspiration for the continuing struggle. For this reason alone, this book is extraordinarily timely.

This is reinforced by the Sandinistas' post-election strategy, which has gradually unfolded as the FSLN adapts itself to the role of opposition party and as the mass organizations which were created after the 1979 revolution work to find a viable identity, role, and form. "*Gobierno de abajo*," the approach called for by outgoing President Daniel Ortega as he prepared for the transition of government on 25 April 1990 to Violeta Barrios de Chamorro, would find continued strength in the imagery of Sandino that filled the streets and roads of Nicaragua. Kent Nosworthy perceptively observes,

> In a small country like Nicaragua—roughly the size of Iowa—history is intimate. Irrespective of class or ideology, the Nicaraguan collective memory bears the indelible stamp of frustration and rage—fueled by generations of U.S. usurpation of the nation's affairs. But that memory also includes a vision of resistance and defiance by Nicaraguan patriots. *Sandinismo* was built upon this vision: these are the feelings and ideas which have motivated the population, first to rise up in insurrection against Somoza, then to defend the nation against counterrevolution, and still today as reconciliation and economic reconstruction move to the top of the agenda.[15]

Sandino in the Streets captures much of the drama, the pathos, the tragedy, and the triumph of the Sandinista revolution. It deserves to be read, seen for its powerful imagery, and absorbed as a compelling chronicle of a revolution.

N O T E S

1. John A. Booth, *The End and the Beginning: The Nicaraguan Revolution,* 2d. edition (Boulder: Westview Press, 1985), pp. 8–9.

2. *Ibid.,* p. 18–19.

3. Hubert Herring, *A History of Latin America from the Beginning to the Present* (New York: Alfred A. Knopf, 1964), p. 462.

4. Sergio Ramírez, *El pensamiento vivo de Sandino* (San José: Editorial Universitaria Centroamericana, 1979), p. xviii, as quoted by Booth, *The End and the Beginning,* p. 32.

5. Herring, *A History of Latin America,* p. 464.

6. Al Burke, *Misery in the Name of Freedom: The United States in Nicaragua, 1909–1988* (Rolling Bay, Washington: Sea Otter Press, 1988), p. 6. The battle of Ocotal in July 1927 between Sandino's forces and the National Guard with the U.S. Marines was the locale of the first organized dive-bombing attack in history. Neill Macaulay, *The Sandino Affair* (Durham: Duke University Press, 1985), p. 81.

7. Booth, *The End and the Beginning,* p. 41.

8. Macaulay, *The Sandino Affair,* p. 53.

9. Macaulay, *The Sandino Affair,* pp. 110–11.

10. Quoted in Burke, *Misery in the Name of Freedom,* p. 6.

11. Dana G. Munro, "The Establishment of Peace in Nicaragua," *Foreign Affairs* XI (July 1933), 699, as quoted by Macaulay, *The Sandino Affair,* p. 240.

12. Booth, *The End and the Beginning,* p. 52.

13. Booth, *The End and the Beginning,* p. 67.

14. Macaulay, *The Sandino Affair,* pp. 8–9.

15. Kent Nosworthy, *Nicaragua: A Country Guide* (Albuquerque: The Inter-Hemispheric Education Resource Center, 1989), p. 5.

The Image of Sandino in the Streets

J O E L   C .   S H E E S L E Y

AUGUSTO CÉSAR Sandino was founder and commander-in-chief of the Army Defending the National Sovereignty of Nicaragua from 1927 to 1933. He was the head of Nicaragua's successful military resistance to occupation by the United States Marines. During this period, Sandino's location, the actions of his army, and his proclamations were all newsworthy. He was sought after for interviews and was photographed whenever possible.

In one of the best known of these photographs Sandino seems to have emerged from a doorway and is standing on the front porch. His left foot is firmly planted with the toe extending forward slightly beyond the edge of the step. He rests his weight on this foot while the other one glides casually to the side. Spurs strapped to his feet accent their direction and placement. He wears tall, laced boots that extend up to just below the knee. Above his boot tops his dark pants billow out loosely only to be gathered in again under his cartridge belt at the waist. He wears a light, large-fitting jacket and loose shirt, both of which are compressed across his chest by a wide strap passing diagonally over his right shoulder. A kerchief is tied neatly around his neck inside the shirt collar. Both arms hang loosely and bend gradually behind his back. A Stetson hat sits squarely on his head, the brim curved up slightly toward the right. A shadow falls across his eyes and forehead.

This Augusto César Sandino photographed sometime in the late 1920s or early 1930s is the Sandino contemporary Nicaraguans remember. Old photographs like this one which document many of the key moments in Sandino's military and political journey have become the basis for the visual expressions of *sandinismo* that fill the streets of Nicaraguan cities and towns.

"Sandino in the streets" is Sandino as image and sign, painted on public and private walls, which are an informal medium of communication in Nicaragua. Reduced to a simple flat silhouette in which his head is lost in the shape of his large brimmed Stetson, a stenciled image of Sandino is like a ghost appearing and reappearing throughout the barrios and districts of Nicaragua. How are these images made? Who paints them? What is their history? How do the Nicaraguan people perceive them? All of these questions play a part in the process of interpreting the images. Their meaning unfolds further in the unique way in which they in turn help us interpret events in Nicaragua.

Images of Sandino which appear in this book are separated by at least fifty years from the accompanying selections from his writing. This comparison of contemporary image with historical writing shows how words and deeds from the past can be transformed into viable symbols for the present. It also demonstrates a sense of continuity in North/South controversies. Sandino would not be a viable symbol today if there were no connections between present and past struggles. The images in this book are not meant to illustrate the text but rather to be read along with it as a contemporary visual transformation of the ethos of Sandino. They demonstrate both the processing of Sandino and the preservation of his image. They are a visual link connecting past and present.

Image and Message

As George Washington or Uncle Sam often provides the backdrop for patriotic messages in the United States, Augusto Sandino does so in Nicaragua. The image of Sandino is a point of convergence for many national and political themes. Calls to patriotism, to defense, to national integrity, to exercise the right to vote, to peace, to production, and to cultural and global awareness have all relied on the image of Sandino for support.

The poignancy of a given image of Sandino often depends on other images with which it is seen. Grouped with Nicaraguan revolutionary heroes such as Nicaraguan poet Rigoberto López Pérez and the intellectual Sandinista Carlos Fonseca, the added presence of Sandino creates a revolutionary trinity. Sandino is read as a military visionary when stencils of him are juxtaposed with stencils of modern Nicaraguan combatants. The appearance on a wall of two hats, Sandino's and the bush hat of the contemporary Nicaraguan soldier, links Sandino's struggle of the past with more recent fighting against the U.S.-sponsored Contras. The standing silhouette of Sandino set within a V-shape composed of a machete and a rifle recalls the prime weapons of Sandino's military force, the Army Defending the National Sovereignty of Nicaragua.

Sandino, however, is much more often associated with peace than with war. His standing silhouette is just as typically supported at the foot with a crisscross of laurel branches as it is with weapons. Frequently he is associated with a dove of peace. In one portrayal he is actually placed within the outline of a bird. The sun is often shown to be rising behind Sandino. Its radiating beams suggest the dawning of a new era.

Sandino was a promulgator of slogans and manifestoes through which he expressed his vision and philosophy, raised the morale of his troops, rallied support among those inclined to join the anti-imperialist struggle, and demonstrated to his opponents that he and his army were full of fighting spirit. Many of these slogans and short statements have been lifted from his manifestoes, letters, and press interviews and are stenciled alongside his image. "Our struggle will triumph because it is the cause of love and justice." "I will not abandon my mountains while there is one Gringo in Nicaragua; I will not abandon my struggle while one of my people's rights remains to be set straight. My cause is the cause of my people, the cause of America, the cause of all oppressed people." These and other phrases and sayings drawn from the writings of Sandino sometimes accompany his image.

Stencils

Stencil makers base their images on a Sandino iconography established through photographs. Artists use reprinted photographs of Sandino as models and cut images as stencils in heavy paper or discarded aluminum lithography plates. Together with a can of spray paint these stencils are templates for endless reproduction of Sandino images.

Sprayed on someone's door, window shutter, a lamppost, or the wall of someone's house or store, stenciled images reduce a portrait of Sandino to an arrangement of flat positive and negative shapes. The viewer connects the shapes to create a meaningful picture. Captured within this picture and acting as its support is the real world onto which it has been painted.

Because stencils are sprayed directly onto the real world, this world is read into the image like a second subject and so influences the image's interpretation. Sprayed onto the surface of a workshop wall, esteem for Sandino rises and falls with the success of the shop. Sprayed onto a tree trunk, he is interpreted within the force of nature itself. An image of Sandino sprayed on the gateposts of a wealthy house means one thing while the same image sprayed on the wall of a peasant's shack suggests something quite different.

Images Before and After the Insurrection

Social and political changes have had a powerful influence both on the significance of images and on the means by which images of Sandino have appeared. Prior to the insurrection of 1979 (when the Sandinistas incorporated nearly all of Nicaragua into their successful overthrow of the Somoza dictatorship) images and slogans in the street were signs of protest. In *La Insurreccion de las paredes* (*The Insurrection of the Walls*) Omar Cabezas relates that prior to the overthrow of 1979, not only was it dangerous to paint the walls with anti-Somoza slogans, but the slogans and images themselves conveyed a sense of warning or danger. In those days painting in the streets was a risky business involving lookouts on the corners along with the painters themselves.

Before the insurrection of 1979 images and slogans in the street gave voice to people who had had no voice and gave a medium to ideas that otherwise could not appear. In those days Somoza and the National Guard were typically the targets of verbal attack in the form of biting slogans; the Sandinista Front for National Liberation (FSLN) was promoted as the much-needed force of liberation. In the midst of conflict, the image of Sandino played a supporting role to immanent messages of the struggle itself.

After the victory of 1979 the context for street art changed. With the oppressive regime of Somoza now removed, the walls became a medium for political discussion of the future of a new Nicaragua. Images and messages centered on how to consolidate revolutionary gains, and promoted notions of nationalism and pride. These messages gained esteem when connected with Sandino, whose 1920s–30s guerrilla struggle represented a model of devotion and sacrifice for country.

The image of Sandino also proved apt for addressing another major issue facing Nicaragua: the displeasure of the United States. As the U.S. became involved in direct attack on Nicaragua through CIA mining of a Nicaraguan harbor, and indirect attacks through an economic blockade and military and financial aid to Contras, the ghost of Sandino was even more loudly recalled from the grave. Sandino, the tireless defender of Nicaraguan sovereignty, became an ever more popular hero. The

battle between North America the giant and Sandino the Central American David was sharply recalled as painted silhouettes of Sandino appeared everywhere.

Today the image of Sandino is an accepted aspect of everyday life, and the clandestine character of the act of stenciling no longer holds. In 1984, the fiftieth anniversary of Sandino's assassination, images of Sandino blossomed all over Nicaragua, appearing as signs of inspiration and commemoration rather than protest. Not only do individuals stencil and paint his image in the street but teams of national and international artists gather to create highly publicized murals in which Sandino and his ideals are often featured.

Authenticity

The propaganda nature of the image of Sandino has caused some to question its authenticity as a true grass-roots expression. The identification of Sandino with the Sandinista Front for National Liberation raises the question whether political indoctrination rather than patriotic ideals is portrayed when Sandino is stenciled in the streets. No doubt both patriotism and political indoctrination have inspired these

images. Changing political conditions warrant varied interpretation of the Sandino image.

When Sandino appeared on Somocista walls he gave expression to a very different sensibility than he did appearing on Sandinista walls. The appearance of Sandino on walls after the 1990 elections yet again takes on new meaning. Sandino is subject to political processing as propaganda because his image ignites Nicaraguan pride. This pride can manifest itself in revolutionary upheaval, but it can also manifest itself in an ordered democratic process. The image of Sandino is authentically related to both. The effort to assign authenticity to one use of Sandino's image and inauthenticity to another is better reconceived as an effort to find the functional meaning of either. Whether stenciled by an organized political group or hand-drawn by a lone artist, the image of Sandino functions as an authentic indigenous focus for forces seeking influence in Nicaragua.

Artists in the Streets

Most of the stenciled images one sees in Nicaragua today are the product of an organized group that has gone out and blitzed one part of town or another with its particular Sandino image or phrase. There are a number of Sandinista agencies and groups that have become involved in stenciling images and messages in the streets. Juventud Sandinista (Sandinista Youth), CDS (Sandinista Defense Committee), CST (Sandinista Labor Union), CPC (Popular Center for Culture), and the womens' organization known as AMNLAE are among a number of organized groups that use stenciling as a means of propaganda and sometimes use the figure of Sandino as part of their message.

Even when Sandino images are produced by organized groups, the images are not necessarily professionally designed. Artists are usually recruited out of the ranks of the group rather than sought outside from among those better trained in drawing. This means that the images produced are striking in their variation. The artists rely on certain trademarks such as the Sandino hat to clearly establish a reference to Sandino and then interpret quite freely and with uneven skill many of the details of his face and posture. The resulting informality places drawing the hero within everyone's reach.

It is not unusual then to find unique hand-drawn images which attest to spontaneous individual expression. Here a young girl draws Sandino stick figures in chalk on the sidewalk, there a boy has drawn Sandino's portrait on his bicep.

Stenciled Sandinos are also open to augmentation by people who come along later and want to add to the Sandino matrix. Many a stenciled silhouette bears a smiling face added by a later painter who confers a sense of silliness on the hero. During the elections of 1984, Liberal Party members often added a bubble emanating from Sandino's mouth containing the words "*Soy Liberal*" (I am a Liberal), referring to Sandino's political affiliation at the beginning of his struggle.

Sometimes alterations to the image besmirch the whole Sandino affair. Whether these alterations are the result of a serious questioning of *sandinismo,* disenchantment with the Sandinistas, or just typical fooling around on the part of school kids, Sandino has nonetheless become the focus of an exchange in which wide participation is welcome.

Sandino in a Collage World

This description of the appearance of the image of Sandino in the streets would not be complete without some consideration given to its decorative quality. It is a quality which would strike fear in the heart of public maintenance departments in most U.S. cities where graffiti are understood to deface the environment. But this fear rises out of defense for the seamless continuity of surface that is the standard in a First World city.

Third World cities offer a widely different environment; what would deface a First World wall may decorate a wall in the Third World. It is not uncommon to find freshly painted walls in Nicaragua where the new paint carefully encircles an area where Sandino had earlier been stenciled. Thus framed, the stencil does assume the status of decoration, its ragged character fitting a cacophonous environment.

Managua has been the center of massive earthquakes, both in Sandino's day and in our own; it has never fully recovered. The central magnet of cathedral and plaza which draws everything to its center is gone from Managua. Like the center of an explosion Managua seems to be pushing everything out from itself. The remains of ruined buildings never repaired from Somoza's day when the quake struck in 1972 rise like tombs out of large, open fields. Added to this is the destruction wrought in the 1979 insurrection when

Somoza used aerial bombing against the Sandinistas. Discontinuity and rupture are commonplace in Managua.

In this environment graffiti are welcome. They help to create a collage world. Graffiti join the overall confrontation of fragments which characterizes both collage and many Third World settings. The feeling of collage dominates one's visual experience in a country where contrasts are more the order than homogeneity. One gets the feeling in Managua that the news is erupting on the walls. And the messages are always changing.

An Aesthetic Interpretation

Perhaps it is within this aesthetic description as much as in a more sociological one that the stencils and hand-painted images of Augusto César Sandino yield their meaning. The impulse among people to draw and stencil images of Sandino in the streets, making a political and artistic statement, is coupled with an impulse to force that expression into everyday life irrespective of the nonexistence of an isolated space reserved for it. The resulting confrontation of fragments is a real-life collage.

In the Third World the confrontation of these fragments is inoffensive because it reflects so well the actual experience of a struggling people, people accustomed to ragged edges and the juxtaposition of dissimilar elements within culture. First and Third World edges raggedly collided as the United States imposed military and economic sanctions against Nicaragua. The graffiti-like fragment of national integrity symbolized in the image of Sandino is appropriately emblazoned here.

The collage nature of this expression of *sandinismo* has important implications for the received meaning of Sandino. Sandino's heroism cannot be mythologized in closed quarters under bureaucratic authority. He is a folk as well as a political hero. He has become a people's as well as a party's symbol. The incipient anarchy of collage in the streets is inimical to bureaucratic consolidation.

Collage of this sort also ruptures any monolithic concept of the hero. Collage opposes uniformity and consolidation. It opposes as well any effort to monumentalize Sandino. He is a rather elusive hero, a ghost woven within layers of peeling paint. A child can sign Sandino's Stetson hat, rolling a figure eight on its side and topping it with a crested mound. At this level Sandino cannot escape the urban or rural reality within which his image is embedded.

His image cannot rise above the real world on huge serenely painted placards as did the image of Stalin or Mao in Communist countries.

The image of Sandino in the streets is a sign. It can be read as artistic expression, historical witness, political propaganda, national honor, even mythical longing. But appearing as it does it is a sign of national health. The image of Sandino remains in the hands of people who insist on using it as a multifaceted matrix in which they can discuss any one of a number of popular concerns. Jeopardized by external and internal pressures this form of discussion may be tenuous at best. It is nevertheless a vital one incorporating traditional ideals with contemporary conflicts.

There is a dynamic bond between these images of Sandino and contemporary Nicaragua. Sandino calls up the ideals of patriotism, independence, and courage; contemporary Nicaragua lives the frustration, conflict, and weariness which are the daily cost of such ideals. The image of Sandino and Nicaragua sustain each other. It is a relationship well characterized by the Nicaraguan slogan *"Sandino vive, la lucha sigue! La lucha sigue, Sandino vive!"*

Sandino lives, the struggle goes on! The struggle goes on, Sandino lives!

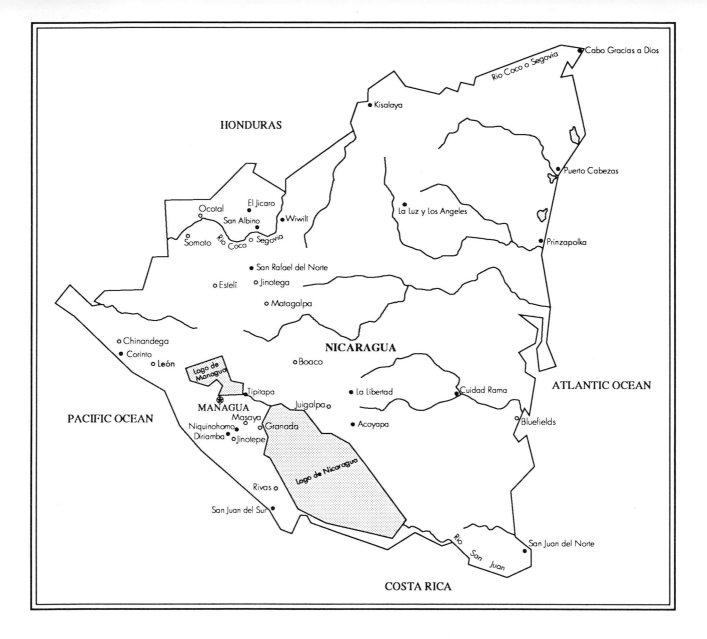

HONDURAS

Cabo Gracias a Dios

Rio Coco o Segovia

Kisalaya

El Jicaro

Ocotal
San Albino
Wiwilí

Somoto
Rio Coco
Segovia

La Luz y Los Angeles

Puerto Cabezas

Prinzapolka

San Rafael del Norte

Estelí
Jinotega

Matagalpa

NICARAGUA

Chinandega
Corinto
León

Lago de
Managua

Boaco

La Libertad

Cuidad Rama

ATLANTIC OCEAN

PACIFIC OCEAN

Tipitapa

MANAGUA
Masaya
Niquinohomo
Diriamba
Jinotepe
Granada

Juigalpa

Acoyapa

Bluefields

Lago de Nicaragua

Rivas

San Juan del Sur

Rio San Juan

San Juan del Norte

COSTA RICA

Origins and Formative Years

1893–1926

Birth and Early Life of Sandino

I was born at four in the morning on the 18th of May, 1895, in the town of La Victoria [Niquinohomo], Department of Masaya, Nicaragua. My parents were two young people under 18 years old. I learned to read in the public schools opened by General J. S. Zelaya, who was constitutional President at that time.

[12, Año IV, No. 65, May 1928, p. 1213] I: 69.

(Related to Nicolás Arrieta in Niquinohomo, November 1933)

My papá entered into an amorous relationship with my mother, who was the servant girl. I do not blame them for this. It is a social reality in Nicaragua that the *patrón* (landowner) or his son makes love with the servant, who goes away to have her baby. There are many other similar social realities.

Afterward, my papá brought me to live with him and I was [my brother] Sócrates' tutor. I took care of him, accompanied him, prepared his horse and put him on it. We played together. . . .

[17, 21 p.] II: 365.

Early Social Consciousness

(Letter to General Pedro Altamirano, March 30, 1931)

I will tell you an anecdote that happened on one of our *haciendas* called Los Angeles when I was only 12 years old. My father is a property owner and I wondered about his taking advantage of peasants' poverty to maintain his financial condition and properties. Understandably my father was surprised when I asked him if he did not consider unjust the way he sustained his small capital.

(July 11, 1893) José Zelaya leads Liberal Party revolt against Roberto Sacasa and becomes president of Nicaragua. (November 20, 1894) Nicaragua re-annexes Atlantic province of La Mosquitia from Great Britain which sends warships to block Puerto Corinto. (May 18, 1895) Augusto César Sandino is born in La Victoria (Niquinohomo), Masaya province. (1896) Liberal Francisco Baca becomes president. (1898) Spanish-American War. U.S. "Rough Riders" invade Cuba. (1899) José Zelaya reelected president.

My father responded that he did not wish to exploit the existing situation of the people, but that if he did not use them, they would be exploited by others.

Well then, it can be said that I began to become conscious of these things at that time.

A short time later I left my home town for adventures in life. I traveled all of our "Central American Isthmus," Mexico, and the United States of America, where I saw all kinds of life. This in truth became my own school.

There are many curious things in my life biography. Not even I knew that I was learning the secrets of human perversity so that later I would tell my brothers the truth, not only in Nicaragua, but also throughout the whole terrestrial globe.

[11, pp. 208–210] II: 164.

(1903) Theodore Roosevelt encourages Panama to separate from Colombia and immediately makes Panama Canal Treaty (November 18). (1905) Roosevelt Corollary to the Monroe Doctrine reinforces U.S. hegemony over Latin America, and Britain gives up claim to the Atlantic Coast of Nicaragua. (1909) U.S. Consul backs José Estrada revolt against Zelaya who had executed two U.S. mercenaries. U.S. Secretary of State Philander Knox breaks relations (December 2) and forces Zelaya out, installing José Madriz as president (December 18).

Emerging Political Awareness (1912)

(Manifesto to the People of the World and Nicaragua, March 13, 1933)

General José Santos Zelaya had to battle with England in order to achieve the reincorporation of the [Atlantic] district of La Mosquitia into Nicaragua. Zelaya was one of the best governors Nicaragua has had in terms of progress and patriotism.

The United States, convinced of Zelaya's strong patriotism and that through him they would not achieve the surrender of Nicaraguan national autonomy, proceeded to stir up the 1909 rebellion in Bluefields. . . . Two North American adventurers surnamed Cannon and Gross, paid by the rebels, mined the river San Juan del Norte to blow up Government troop ships. Under General Salvador Toledo, government troops shot these two adventuresome yankees.

The United States then demanded that

(May 19, 1910) U.S. Marines land in Bluefields and declare this port city a "neutral zone to protect U.S. business interests." *(August 28, 1910)* José Estrada deposes President Madriz.

Zelaya lay down the Presidency of the Republic and tried to capture him, but the president of Mexico, don Porfirio Díaz, provided a warship to save Zelaya from ferocious Uncle Sam. The rebellion, headed by Adolfo Díaz, Juan B. Estrada, José M. Moncada, and Emiliano Chamorro, later came to power and consummated the criminal Bryan-Chamorro Treaties.

. . . . The revolution of 1912 culminated in the assassination of the undefeated and glorious General Benjamín Zeledón. I was a kid of 17 when I witnessed the massacre of Nicaraguans in Masaya and other places in the Republic by the North American filibuster forces. I personally observed the body of Benjamín Zeledón, who was buried in Catarina, near my home town. The death of Zeledón gave me the key to understanding our national situation in the face of North American freebooting.

[17, 25 p.] II: 304–306.

(October 26, 1910) *U.S. imposes the Dawson Pact, giving U.S. economic and political hegemony in Nicaragua.* **(January 1, 1911)** *Estrada and Adolfo Díaz installed as president and vice-president. Palace coup replaces Estrada with Díaz (May 9).*

Moral and Intellectual Growth

(Letter to Froylán Turcios, April 1, 1928)

During my stay away from my native land I was never tranquil in spirit. . . . I confess that in this secular world I never found happiness, and so, in search of spiritual consolation, I read many mythological books and sought religious teachers. The last of these was the honorable señor Barbiauz, who lives in Alamo, Veracruz, Mexico.

I have always been inclined to read all that in my judgment is moral and instructive. One of the things I have seen clearly in my most recent observations is that men to whom God has given a great mind frequently become arrogant. I cannot understand why they forget they are mortals and fall into the unpardonable crime of trafficking with injustice and treating human beings as if they were a herd of pigs. This is the vile end of 95 percent of my fellow citizens.

I have come to understand that sound knowledge is either scorned or invoked by unscrupulous men only to get soft jobs, without regard to humanity or God.

In summary, I deduce from my learning that humans cannot live with dignity apart from sound reason and the laws marked by honor.

For this reason, and since the United States of North America, exercising the right only of brute force, presumes to take away our Native Land and our Liberty, I have accepted this unjustified challenge against our territorial sovereignty. I take responsibility for my actions before the witness of history. To remain inactive or indifferent, as do the majority of my fellow citizens, would be to join up with the great multitude of those who sell out and kill our nation.

. . . . I love justice and will sacrifice myself for it. Material treasures do not hold power over me. The treasures I long for are spiritual.

[12, Año IV, No. 65, May 1928, p. 1213] I: 69–70.

Reflections on Experiences Abroad

(1922)

My dearest papá:

In these past months I have been able to save some money, but at the cost of some privation. I dream of going to more civilized countries, where, if I am not able to make money, at least I will gain a broader and clearer view of civilization and achieve something.

This place is picturesque and much money is to be made, but what isn't lost in sighs goes in tears. Listen. Life here is completely bohemian and the climate itself is truly a source of infections. Thus workers here lose money either because

---

*(**June 6, 1911**) Castillo-Knox Treaty gives Nicaraguan banks, railroads, and customs as collateral. (**July 29, 1912**) Díaz calls in U.S. Marines to put down rebellion. This begins a ten-year U.S. military occupation. (**October 4, 1912**) Gen. Benjamín Zeledón is de-feated in Masaya and is executed by U.S. Marines. (**January 1913**) Woodrow Wilson is inaugurated as president in U.S. and Adolfo Díaz in Nicaragua.*

of frequent illnesses or because they are unable to control their disorderly passions.

. . . . You have to understand how hard it is to go to another country with little money. When you disembark, you have thousands of different impressions and everything looks strange. No one speaks to you; without money you are nothing. After seeking a hotel, you dress in your best and set out for a job. They look you over from head to foot, ask a thousand questions, what you can do and why you left where you were. They even insult you. You see now why one has to arrive with money, rather than without it and looking outlandish.

Here exist thousands of men who wish to return to their homes but are not able. They don't have a way, because even though they earn hundreds of dollars, they waste it. Here, wherever one goes, one hears music of all kinds, great dances, much merrymaking—today among some and tomorrow, others. The ones who

(August 5, 1914) Bryan-Chamorro Treaty gives U.S. the right to a canal across Nicaragua for $3 million. The Panama Canal is finished this year. (January 1, 1917) Emiliano Chamorro is inaugurated as president of Nicaragua. (1919) Treaty of Versailles ends World War I.

profit are the owners of the innumerable cantinas and gaming houses. This life is not for a man who wants to distinguish himself in something. For this reason I do everything I can to leave as soon as possible.

Greetings to my brothers and stepmother, and a strong embrace from your untiring but miserable AUGUSTO.

[17, 2 p.] I: 73–74.

I have a number of recommendations from the different corporations where I gave my service that bear witness to my honorable conduct. It was as a mechanic that I distinguished myself.

[12, Año IV, No. 65, May 1928, p. 1213] I: 69–70.

Growing Awareness of Nationalism

It was in Mexico, where I was employed by a yankee firm, the Huasteca Petroleum

(January 1, 1921) Diego M. Chamorro becomes Nicaraguan president. *(1924)* The U.S. announces withdrawal of the Marines after November elections. Conservative Carlos Solorzano and Liberal Juan Sacasa are elected.

Company, that I realized that I should return to Nicaragua to take part in the struggle against the North American influence. . . . By the year 1925, I concluded that everything had turned to shame in Nicaragua. The men of that land had completely lost honor. At that same time, due to my sincere character, I was able to surround myself with a group of spiritual friends. We discussed daily among ourselves the Latin American submission to the hypocritical and forceful advance of the assassin yankee empire.

One day I expressed to my friends that if there were a hundred men in Nicaragua who loved her as much as I, our nation would restore its absolute sovereignty. My friends responded that possibly there would be this number of men or more, but the difficulty would be in identifying them. From that moment on I desired to find these hundred legitimate sons of Nicaragua.

[1, pp. 35–38] I: 79–80.

*(**August 4, 1925**) U.S. Marines withdraw from Nicaragua. (**October 25, 1925**) Forces of Emiliano Chamorro seize Loma Fortress in Managua. (**January 16, 1926**) Under pressure from Chamorro, Solorzano renounces and flees, along with Sacasa. Chamorro is proclaimed president but the* *U.S. refuses to recognize him. (**May 2, 1926**) The Constitutionalist War erupts as Liberals and Conservatives clash in Atlantic Coast. U.S. Marines land again.*

Return to Nicaragua

SANDINO JOINS THE
CONSTITUTIONALIST STRUGGLE

1926–1927

Return to Nicaragua

(1926)

The intervention of the United States in Nicaragua has caused the rest of the people of Central America and Mexico to hate us, the Nicaraguans. I had the opportunity to confirm this hatred in my travels through these countries. I felt profoundly wounded when they would call me "nation-seller," "shameless," and "traitor." At first I would reply to these accusations that, not being a man of state, I didn't consider myself worthy of these dishonorable titles. But then after reflection I realized they were right, because as a Nicaraguan I had the right to protest.

I found out that a revolutionary movement had broken out in Nicaragua. I was working at the Huasteca Petroleum Company in Tampico. It was the 15th of May, 1926. I had savings that amounted to five thousand dollars. I took three thousand

---

(May 6, 1926) Sandino resigns from the Huasteca Petroleum Co. He arrives in Nicaragua on June 1 and begins work as assistant paymaster at the San Albino gold mine in Nueva Segovia.

dollars and came to Managua. I informed myself of what was happening and went to the mines of San Albino, emerging into active political life, whose details everyone knows.

[3, pp. 89–90] I: 81.

Sandino's Column Joins Constitutionalist Revolt

When I left Mexico to return to this privileged land, my spirit still was not aware of the terrible and heavy task that awaited me. Events were giving me the key to the attitude that I should assume as a legitimate son of Nicaragua. In the face of the capitulation and cowardice of our political leaders, I would represent the spirit of our people.

My good faith, my worker simplicity, and my patriot's heart received the first political surprise when, after having engaged in battle with the interventionists in the

---

(August 1926) Gen. José María Moncada arrives in Puerto Cabezas to direct the Constitutionalist Army in opposition to Chamorro. (October 10–30, 1926) U.S. attempt at truce aboard the USS Denver ends in failure. Fighting continues.

14

15

Segovias, I went to seek arms in Puerto Cabezas. Our Constitutional Government under Dr. Juan Bautista Sacasa had been set up there. I spoke with him and was told my case would be taken up with General Moncada. Moncada refused roundly, and I remained in that port forty days being put off, because the ministers of Sacasa were full of presidential ambitions.

During that time, on the 24th of December, 1926, the North American pirates forced Sacasa to remove his troops and war materials from Puerto Cabezas within 24 hours. Sacasa couldn't remove the weapons and the pirates sank them in the bay. His Honor Guard left in disarray by land and sea to Prinzapolka, leaving Sacasa and his ministers under siege, encircled by the yankee army tents. I followed behind Sacasa's Guard with six men and a group of local prostitutes who helped us recover rifles and ammunition amounting to thirty rifles and seven thousand cartridges.

(October 26, 1926) Sandino proselytizes mine workers, buys some guns, and arms a small band to join the constitutionalist struggle. (October 30, 1926) Without U.S. recognition, Chamorro resigns. (November 11, 1926) Nicaraguan Congress elects conservative Adolfo Díaz president.

17

The ineptness of our political leaders was greater than expected and it was then that I understood that the sons of our people were without leaders and that new men were needed.

[5, pp. 126–135] II: 238.

Colonel Salvador Bosque Joins Sandino

The morning was cloudy and cold. The houses of Puerto Cabezas looked sad after the torrential downpour the night before. The little boat in which my five companions and I traveled was tied up at the port authority dock.

We jumped to the dock and in the fog discovered some men armed with new carbines and bullet-belts. They were not dressed as soldiers, but rather looked like Mexican peasants. . . .

A young man of about 35, olive-

Díaz is immediately recognized by the U.S. Sacasa is backed by Mexico. (November–December, 1926) After a defeat at El Jícaro, Sandino's Segovian Column goes down river to Puerto Cabezas, Atlantic Coast, to seek weapons from the Constitutionalist Army.

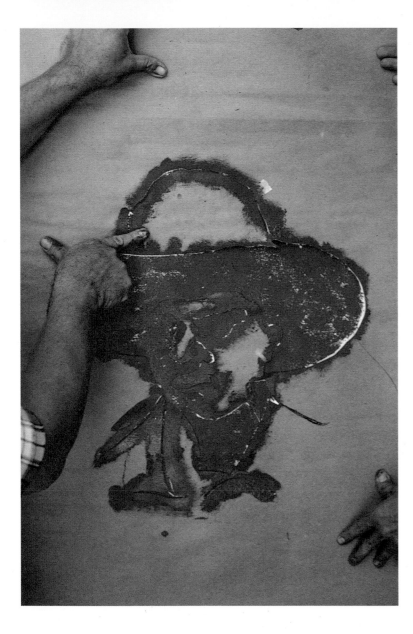

complexioned with black eyes and eyebrows that joined, walked about the dock slowly, occasionally tapping his boot with his whip. Of regular height, with thick, trimmed beard, he was dressed in a khaki riding habit, a wide-brimmed hat, and high boots and had a red and black kerchief around his neck. I told him I was the head of a revolutionary column that operated in the Segovias and that I wished to see Dr. Sacasa. He accompanied us to the presidential house. This youth was a colonel in Sacasa's army and a native of Diriamba. His name was Salvador Bosque.

On February 2 we returned to the Segovias, with some arms, accompanied by some new companions, among whom was Colonel Salvador Bosque. . . . Colonel Bosque became the First Chief of the Second Company of our famous cavalry that spread such terror among the enemy. Our column went from triumph to triumph, controlling valleys, towns, and cities.

(December 24, 1926) *U.S. Marines declare Puerto Cabezas a "neutral zone," destroy weapons, and give Sacasa 48 hours to withdraw. The Marines occupy Bluefields, Río Grande, and Prinzapolka.*

Those regions where our column operated are very beautiful and our forces were received with sympathy because all the inhabitants are revolutionaries and make common cause with us.

[2, pp. 25–27] I: 401–403.

Fighting for the Constitutionalist Army

Returning to the Segovias on February 2, 1927, I found that the Conservatives had destroyed General Francisco Parajón's forces in Chinandega, which sought refuge in El Salvador.

Full of enthusiasm, the Segovian men awaited us in El Chipote. Into their hands I put the 30 rifles and 7,000 cartridges. Two days later we put them to use in our first triumph in San Juan. Following this we routed the enemy from Ocotal. We agreed with López Irías that he would oc-cupy Estelí and that my men and I would take Jinotega.

López Irías augmented his column rapidly and a few days later he surprised the enemy in Chagagüillo and captured their war convoy. But the enemy returned with more strength and disorganized his column, making him flee to Honduras.

The enemy occupied Estelí and Jinotega. Our Segovian Column was the only Liberal column in the west or north, and we were undaunted in San Rafael del Norte, in spite of being surrounded.

. . . . The enemy had free run in all the interior and accumulated his strength by defeating our Constitutionalist forces that moved up from the Atlantic under Generals Luis Beltrán Sandoval and José María Moncada. . . . On my part, I would have rushed to save Moncada and his men from their desperate situation, but my column was relatively small and we were fighting daily. Nevertheless, from Chipote

---

(January 6, 1927) New contingent of Marines disembarks in Puerto Corinto on Pacific side. (February 2, 1927) Sandino's small band returns to the Segovias with thirty rifles and wins battle in San Juan de Segovia. (February 9, 1927) U.S. mercenary pilots bomb Chinandega. The Ma-rines declare the Managua-León-Chinandega railroad a "neutral zone." (February 25, 1927) U.S. sells 3,000 rifles and 200 machine guns with 3 million rounds to Díaz government.

I sent 150 men with eight poor rifles under Colonels Simón Cantarero and Pompilio Reyes. I gave them instructions to offer their services to General Moncada and wait for me.

Our forces departed for Jinotega. At five o'clock in the morning we surrounded the plaza. Its white walls and pallid lights were blanketed with a fog illumined by the first rays of the sun. For an instant the sweet calm in which Jinotega slept detained us. A few minutes later the bloody combat started. It terminated at five in the afternoon with the triumph of our liberating guns. The enemy felt the full impact of war.

Our Segovian Column was made up now of 800 cavalrymen well equipped, and our red-and-black banner was raised over those wild, cold hills.

[5, pp. 126–135] II: 239–240.

On the Eve of Victory, Moncada Capitulates in Stimson Agreement

On the 11th of March, I left with my Army for General Moncada's camp. Luck was with me and in El Bejuco my Army broke the chains restraining the revolution. . . . The decisive moment was near. The final bells had tolled for Conservativism, seeing that the Liberal Army had 7,000 well-equipped men full of enthusiasm while the Conservative Army only counted on a thousand-plus men willing to fight. Their men were deserting, so triumph was ours on every front.

We had won, but just as we were ready to make the last push and victoriously enter the capital city, Managua, the Barbarian Colossus of the North proposed to General Moncada an armistice for 48 hours to seek peace. The [Conservative] government forces were losing and there were [U.S.] commitments to Adolfo Días.

[11, pp. 39–41] I: 107–109.

---

*(**March 7, 1927**) Gen. Logan Feland arrives to command 2,000 Marines.*
*(**April 13–19, 1927**) Sandino's victorious troop swells to 800. Moncada tries to rid himself of Sandino.*

All but One

(May 1927)

I found Moncada lying in a hammock that had been strung under a shade tree. He greeted me, making himself comfortable in the hammock and arranging a gold cross from the North American Marines that he wore on a white ribbon around his neck.

. . . . He returned from Tipitapa with the [Stimson] agreement and the promise to become president in his pocket. . . . Moncada had sold the Liberal Army, of which he was the general in charge, like a pair of oxen. . . .

I told Moncada again that I would be one of the opposition. . . . He tried to soft-talk me into accepting the cease-fire. He assured me that it would be crazy to fight against the United States of the North because it is a very powerful nation with 120

(April 17, 1927) Envoy Henry Stimson arrives from Washington to mediate. *(May 4, 1927)* In Tipitapa, Moncada and Stimson declare a truce, which Sandino disagrees with.

26

million inhabitants. I could do nothing
with 300 men under my command. What
would happen would be like what happens to a little lamb in the grasp of a tiger:
"The more it moves, the more the tiger
sinks its claws into the lamb's flesh."

From that moment I felt a profound contempt for Moncada. I told him that I consider it a responsibility to die for Liberty.
("Liberty or Death" is the motto of the
Red and Black Flag which I had raised.) I
told him the people expect liberty as a
result of the Constitutionalist War. He
smiled sarcastically and told me: "No,
man, . . . how are you going to sacrifice
yourself for the people? The people are
not grateful. I tell you from my own experience that . . . life will end and the nation will continue. The responsibility of
every human being is to enjoy life and live
well, without worrying too much. . . ."

I led General Moncada to believe that I
had considered the matter and was re-

*(May 8, 1927) The Liberal generals surrender without waiting for Sandino. The Stimson agreement gives amnesty and the U.S. pays $10 for
every surrendered rifle. Sandino leaves for Jinotega on May 13. Moncada
is made vice-president under Díaz.*

solved to second the opinion of the rest of the commanders, but that I wanted him to permit me to surrender my arms in the city of Jinotega. . . .

When I arrived in Jinotega there was great enthusiasm when they saw us with all our weapons and perhaps even better equipped than when we had left. . . . They gave us many flowers. I received many photographs of young ladies dedicated to me. . . . The second night I proceeded to send several machine guns, six hundred rifles, and a large quantity of ammunition with some men to the Segovian mountains.

[3, pp. 90–91; 9, pp. 222–226] I: 96–101.

(May 15, 1927) *The disarmed Liberal troops are received with joy in Managua. Sandino's troops go to San Rafael del Norte. Díaz asks U.S. to supervise upcoming elections.* **(May 18, 1927)** *Sandino marries Blanca Aráuz in San Rafael del Norte and shortly leaves with his troops.*

The Girl from San Rafael Del Norte

(May 18, 1927)

I met Blanca Aráuz, telegraph operator of the town of San Rafael del Norte. She was a pleasing 19-year-old girl.

My officers and I had been staying in Blanca's house, where the telegraph office was also located. Long hours day and night I had remained in front of the telegraph desk where Blanca worked. My telegraph messages were many. . . . In this manner I fell in love with Blanca and she became my fiancée. . . .

The 18th of May I reached 32 years of age, and this same day I contracted marriage with Blanca in the Cathedral of San Rafael del Norte. At two in the morning of the 18th, I went to the temple with Blanca and our godfathers, accompanied by the family. Six of my aides accompanied us to the church. The townspeople did not know that we were getting married.

At that hour the weather was cold and foggy. We found the church profusely illuminated. I breathed the fragrance of the incense. The burning candles and the perfumes that filled the air reminded me of my childhood.

The priest invited me to confession. I confessed sincerely. The godfathers kneeled with us at the altar. Blanca had on a white dress, a veil, and a tiara made of orange and lemon flowers. I had my pistols in my belt and I was dressed in a riding uniform of coffee-colored gabardine, and high dark boots.

We left the church and in the street I felt like a new man. I seemed to be walking on air. . . . On the street corner were some of my young men, who congratulated us as we passed. When we entered Blanca's house there were sounds throughout the town of rifle and pistol shots and machine-gun rounds. It was done without my permission, but I understood my lads were motivated by enthusiasm and I didn't say anything. Everywhere we could hear enthusiastic "vivas" and we received innumerable congratulations.

. . . . Two days later I left my wife to intern myself in the Segovian jungles, where I have remained fighting in defense of the honor of my Homeland.

[16, 2 p.] I: 102–104.

Sandino Forms His Own Resistance in the Mountains

May to October 1927

Reply to General José M. Moncada

(circa May 23, 1927)

To José María Moncada.

I do not know why you wish to give me orders now. I remember that you always mistrusted me when you were Commander-in-Chief. You never wanted to give me the troops I requested to combat the enemy. And when Dr. Sacasa gave me 45 men and weapons, you were displeased. It seems you were jealous of me.

Undoubtedly you are aware of my temperament and know that I am unbreakable. Now I want you to come and disarm me. I am here and wait for you. Otherwise, you will not make me give up. *I do not sell myself, nor do I surrender;* you have to conquer me. I plan to fulfill my duty and I hope that my protest written with blood remains for the future.

[9, pp. 240–241] I: 111.

(May 21, 1927) U.S. troops occupy Jinotega. Moncada sets up his head-quarters there and telegraphs Sandino demanding surrender.

Moncada Sends Sandino's Father to Seek His Surrender

(May 23, 1927)

Moncada enlisted my father to go to San Rafael del Norte to convince me that I should surrender. In San Rafael del Norte I had only twenty-nine cavalrymen, with four machine guns.

. . . . . On the 23rd, we arrived at Yalí, where I received a telegram sent by Blanca telling me that my father was in San Rafael del Norte. She implored me in his name and hers that I await him in Yalí because he wanted to see me and embrace me before I went into the mountains.

I acceded to her request and we halted the march. At three in the afternoon my father's arrival was announced. I went into the street to receive him. A group of about ten men on good mounts came into sight. In the midst of those ex-members

(May 22, 1927) Ex-president Juan B. Sacasa goes to Costa Rica. **(May 23, 1927)** *Sandino's father sent by Moncada to urge surrender, which he refuses to do. Some men leave Sandino.*

of my Column, the figure of an olive-skinned, medium-sized man stood out. He was dressed in a blue cashmere suit, a straw hat with a black grosgrain band, and a bow tie of the same color. That man was my father.

His first words were a supplication on his behalf, my mother's and my family's, not to make armed resistance to the yankee invaders. He told me he was sorry about the surrender of the Liberal Army and that if all the leaders of our Constitutionalist Army had adopted the attitude that I had tried to take, Nicaragua would have saved itself from humiliation. But none had, and, if I didn't desist from my purposes, I would have to succumb fruitlessly, as had General Benjamín Zeledón in 1912 when the yankees attacked the Plaza de Masaya, defended by the hitherto undefeated general.

I replied that the attitude I was trying to take was none other than the one General Benjamín Zeledón had taken at that time.

When my father saw in me the firm purpose to sacrifice myself, I comprehended in this moment that he felt greater affection for me, and he said:

"If you are resolved to sacrifice yourself, you should do it with all honor. After firing the first shot against the invader, you have nothing left to hope for except death or victory. You should never back down with weak pretexts like hunger, sleepless nights, or weariness. In these cases, it is better to commit suicide rather than to fall into shameful surrender."

Night came and we stopped talking about giving up and only talked of family matters and reminisced about neighbors of our home town.

That night I slept like a baby. When I awoke on the 24th, I received another disillusion. Eight of my twenty-nine men had requested leave, and had gone to their homes. Now on the 24th it was not twenty-nine but twenty-one men in my

Column, and it looked like I might remain all alone.

[16, 9 p.] II: 411–415.

Sandino Resolves to Continue Struggle

Yalí, 23rd of May, 1927.
To Local Authorities in all the Departments

My esteemed sirs:

The republics of Argentina, Brazil, and Chile have requested of the North American State Department to act as judges of the affairs of Nicaragua. The State Department accepted. This [commission] will overturn Sacasa and Díaz and propose a Liberal government. My resolution is this: *I am not willing to surrender my arms even if all others do. I will die with the few that accompany me because it is better to die as rebels than live as slaves. . . .*

Meanwhile, I remain here, waiting for the determination of Colonel Stimson regarding our affair.

Patria y Libertad.

A. C. Sandino

[11, pp. 39–41] I: 107–109.

Manifesto To Nicaraguans, Central Americans, and the Indio-Hispanic Race

(July 1, 1927)

A man who does not demand even a handful of earth for his sepulcher deserves to be heard, and not only to be heard but also to be believed.

I am a Nicaraguan and I feel proud because in my veins circulates, above everything else, Indian blood, which by atavism includes the mystery of being a patriot, loyal and sincere.

I am a workman, but my idealism abounds on the wide horizon of internationalism, which represents the right to be free and to do justice, even though to achieve justice it might be necessary to shed blood. . . .

The oligarchy will say that I am a plebeian. It does not bother me. My major honor is to have come from the bosom of the oppressed, who are the soul and nerve of the Race.

Pessimists will say that we are very small to undertake a job of this magnitude. To the contrary, I judge and am persuaded that however insignificant we might be, our pride and our patriot hearts are greater. For that reason, in the presence of the Homeland and history, I swear that my sword will defend the national honor and it will bring redemption to the oppressed.

I accept the challenge by the cowardly colossal invader and by the traitors of our Native Land. Our chests will be the ramparts upon which their hordes will be

---

(June 5, 1927) Marines occupy San Rafael del Norte, as Sandino fades into Segovian jungle to El Jícaro, where he sets up quarters. (June 19, 1927) Sandino appoints Francisco Estrada as political chief and sends a notice to all Segovian authorities. (June 30, 1927) Sandino's little troop occupies the U.S.-owned San Albino mine in Nueva Segovia. (July 1, 1927) Sandino writes a manifesto to all Latin Americans about his resistance to the occupation and calls for solidarity.

broken. I have the firm conviction that when they have killed the last of my soldiers, more than a battalion of them will have bitten the dust in my uncultivated mountains. . . .

I want to have the satisfaction of convincing my fellow patriots, the Central Americans, and the Indio-Hispanic Race that in the Andean mountain range there is a group of patriots who will know how to die as men, in open fight, defending the national honor.

Patria y Libertad.

[16, 4 p.] I: 117–120.

U.S. Marine Captain Hatfield Labels Sandino a Bandit

(received July 11, 1927)

General Augusto C. Sandino, El Jícaro.

It seems impossible that you remain deaf to our reasonable proposals, yet in spite of your insolent replies, I again give you an opportunity to surrender. As you doubtless know, we are prepared to attack your positions and terminate you and your forces, once and for all, if you insist in sustaining yourself.

Moreover, if you manage to escape to Honduras or any other part, a price will be put on your head and never will you be able to return to your country which you pretend to love so much. Rather, as a bandit you will flee from your own peaceful countrymen. But if you come to Ocotal with your forces and give up your weapons, you and your soldiers will have guarantees that I give, representing a great powerful nation that doesn't win battles by treason. . . .

Then you will be able to live an honorable life in your homeland, with the possibility of helping your fellow citizens today and tomorrow. Otherwise, you will be an exile and outlaw, like a pig, hunted down and repudiated everywhere, awaiting your shameful death. . . . No outlaw has prospered or died contentedly. As an example of one like you, who retraced his steps in time, I remind you of Aguinaldo of the Philippines, who afterward was a splendid friend of the United States.

Finally, I inform you that Nicaragua has had its last revolution. Soldiers of fortune will not have more opportunity to employ their talents in the future. I await you in Ocotal at eight in the morning of the 14th of July, 1927. Your decision will save the lives of many of your followers and your own. Your answer will be *yes* or *no*. Thus let it be.

G. D. Hatfield

[16, 3 p.] I: 127–128.

(July 2, 1927) Gen. Julian Latimer sends 300 armed men to apprehend Sandino. President Coolidge names Frank McCoy president of Nicaraguan National Election Board. (July 8, 1927) Admiral D. F. Sellers replaces Latimer as commander of Special Services Squadron in Nicaragua.

(July 11, 1927) Marine Captain G. D. Hatfield orders Sandino to surrender or suffer the consequences.

39

Sandino Responds to Hatfield Ultimatum

El Rempunjón, 12 of July, 1927

Mr. G. D. Hatfield:

When I joined the Constitutionalist movement, I did so with the firm purpose of achieving *Free Homeland or Death.* Since we have not yet achieved liberty, nor have I died, I will continue in our firm objective of fighting you. We will not surrender our weapons, because they represent the energetic protest of my Native Land, and for this reason your threats are pale to me and it doesn't matter a bit whom you represent. The first to cross the frontier we have established will leave several tons of dead bodies on the battlefield. If you are resolved, you can come any hour and thus we will have the honor of irrigating the soil of the Native Land with traitors' and invaders' blood.

Furthermore, if the United States wants

peace in Nicaragua, it should allow a legitimate Nicaraguan as president, elected by the people. Then I will put down my arms peacefully without the need for anyone to impose it.

[16, 3 p.] I: 129.

Captain Hatfield Publicly Outlaws Sandino

(circa July 13, 1927)

To all whom it may interest:

Augusto C. Sandino, at one time a General of the Liberal Armies, is now an individual outside the law, in rebellion against the Government of Nicaragua. Therefore, those who travel with him or remain in territory occupied by his forces do so at their own risk. Neither the Government of Nicaragua nor that of the United States of America will be responsible for the dead or wounded that might result from

44

the military operations of the Nicaraguan or American forces in the territory occupied by Sandino.

G. D. Hatfield,
Capt. Marine Corps,
Commandant of Nueva Segovia

[11, pp. 47–49] I: 121–122.

Sandino Defies Captain Hatfield

(July 12, 1927)

El Chipote Camp, by way of San Fernando

To Captain G. D. Hatfield,
El Ocotal

I received your communication yesterday and I understand it. I will not surrender and I await you here. I desire free homeland or death. I do not fear you. I count on the ardor of patriotism in those who accompany me.

(July 15–27, 1927) *Battle of Ocotal lasts 15 hours, and U.S. airplanes strafe and bomb the city. Sandino retreats strategically and attacks San Fernando and Los Capules, Nueva Segovia.*

Patria y Libertad.

A. C. Sandino

[11, pp. 47–49] II: 121.

Who Are the Real Bandits?

What right have the foreign troops to call us bandits and to say that we are the aggressors? We are in our own house. . . .

We owe everything to the enemy. If they had not attacked us, our condition would be miserable. We have taken from them all that we have. If they had not attacked us, we would not have clothing nor munitions, and we would have perished, because we do not know how to live like bandits.

We have not taken anything away from the peasants. In El Chipote, the peasants brought cattle and food right to the trenches for our men. We have lacked nothing. Do you think that if we were

(August 8, 1927) U.S. Intelligence reports that "Sandino cannot cause more problems." (September 2, 1927) Establishment of the Army Defending the National Sovereignty of Nicaragua, in El Chipote headquarters.

48

bandits we could have resisted for a year and a half in a fortified position like this, against the immense power of the United States? No one would protect us if we were bandits. The enemy says, "It should end soon, he has no munitions, nor arms, nor food." But the enemy forgets that the people of Nicaragua maintain us. The enemy forgets that he himself supplies us with munitions and arms. . . .

We are no more bandits than Washington was. If the American people had not become debilitated in terms of justice and elemental human rights, they would not so easily forget their past, when a handful of ragged soldiers marched over the snow, leaving bloody footprints behind, in order to gain liberty and independence.

If their consciences had not been hardened by material riches, the Americans would not forget so easily that a nation, however weak it may be, sooner or later obtains its liberty. Each abuse of power

hastens the destruction of him who exercises it. We will go toward the sun of liberty or toward death. And if we die, our cause will continue to live. Others will follow us.

[13, Año XI, No. 571. 1928, p. 17]
I: 237, 240–241.

Occupation of the
San Albino Gold Mine

(circa July 14, 1927)

To my fellow Nicaraguans.

Chas. Butters, an American who calls himself owner of the San Albino mine, defrauds my fellow citizens whom he obliges to work 12 hours a day. He pays them with vouchers worth from 5 pesos to 5 cents, which are accepted only in his commissary in exchange for double-priced merchandise. *He believes that he is authorized by his nationality* to commit these

---

(September 9, 1927) Battle of Las Flores initiates new offensive by Sandino. (September 19) Battle of Telpaneca.

abuses, and gets by with them. To be American is not to be exempt, and the legitimate people have their law and justice to prevent these abuses. . . .

Moncada has myopic ignorance about the difficult social problem of his fellow citizens who, extorted and harassed, demand justice hitherto denied to them. Every foreigner that transgresses or commits reprehensible acts falls under the sanction of the law and has to suffer the consequences, and even more so if the country is at war.

The gold produced from the bowels of Nicaraguan soil is Nicaraguan and is extracted by Nicaraguan workers' hands. Where, then, is the backing for the enormous debt of $45,000 dollars in vouchers held by workers who live from hand to mouth and who can be fired without notice with only worthless stamped paper in their pockets? How will Chas. Butters redeem this sacred debt owed to the miserable, semi-nude, malaria-weakened worker who doesn't have fare to go home because his savings are in paper worth nothing outside the mine?

Moncada, the people know what is just, and when justice is denied they take it. Since I am of the people and I know law and justice, I have done justice in the name of the people, appropriating these properties that belong to the nation, to convert this debt. I am paying [the workers] with the same gold that the company produces.

Once this is done, its properties will be returned to the swindling company, if indeed the people can be shown that it is the legitimate owner.

Patria y Libertad.

A. C. Sandino

[16, 3 p.] I: 123–125.

Love of Country is Above All Loves

El Chupón, 6th of October, 1927

My sweet wife:

Today I received your letter of August 15 which gives me more pleasure than you imagine. I don't know how to respond to your lamentations. . . . I know that I don't make you happy, but let me say that when I proposed marriage I was inspired by the greatest desire to love you with all my heart. Never did I imagine that circumstances would make me cause you to be distraught nor that your desperation would become so great that you could think of suicide. Even though you say that I do not love you, I long to convince you that in spite of the great love I have for you, it is possible to sacrifice oneself as we are now doing. We who, with rifle on shoulder, are defending with desperation our rights as free men understand that we could never accept a yoke of cowardly slavery.

I prefer to lose your love and die in open battle against the assassin invader than to permit that you and I, and our children—should we have any—survive in an oppression that only cowards and the irresolute are able to accept. I place above all loves the love of my country, and you must come to realize that to be happy—for us to be happy—it is necessary that the sun of liberty shine on our country. . . .

Be optimistic, have faith in God, and he will help us free ourselves, so that tomorrow, when we are together and this same God gives us a baby, he will bless the memory of his father, who, with unbreakable will, has prepared for him: Patria y Libertad. . . .

I suppose there is no doubt about our triumph, because God has not only favored our cause, but also has become an interested party to it. . . .

Blanca mine, receive a million kisses and a flood of embraces until I have the pleasure of holding you in my arms personally.

Yours,

A. C. Sandino

[16, 2 p.] I: 155–156.

Offensive by Sandino's Army

THE "BANDIT" PHASE

October 1927 to February 1928

Yankee Savagery

(To Froylán Turcios, January 1928)

The town of Quilalí, set on fire by the conquistadors, has burned for three days. One by one the houses have been reduced to ashes. It has disappeared from the map of Nicaragua, burned by the criminal hand of the adventurers who are destroying our sovereignty. . . . Everything they encountered in their path has been reduced to ashes. The work and sacrifices of humble peasants are destroyed by the horde of invaders. Hundreds of young ladies and respectable matrons have been violated. Many of them perished after resisting, assassinated by those who try to convince the world that they are not trying to subdue our country.

For these tremendous crimes by these human brutes there is hate, much hate, holy hate by Nicaraguan patriots. Yankee savagery will not encounter any mercy while Sandino lives. His incensed Army will fight until it throws these adventurers out of the territory.

[12, Año IV, No. 59, February 1928, p. 1123] I: 218–219.

Enemy Forces Move Toward El Chipote Stronghold

(November, 1927)

We lay in ambush with machine guns in the trenches. The enemy arrived and we opened fire. It was a frightful slaughter. The pirates fell like leaves from the trees. We were invisible, well protected, and had few losses. After the first encounter we laid ambushes for the reinforcement columns in Trincheras, Varillal, and Plan Grande.

We met three more times in Las Cruces, where the last battle lasted four days, until we could regroup in El Chipote. The enemy lost six hundred men. We lost some thirty. In the fight we captured a North American flag. . . .

There also died Capt. Livingston, column leader, on whom we found day-orders, documents, and maps. . . . In Las Cruces pirate Capt. Bruce died, who had wired his mother in the United States, "By the first of January we will have cut off the head of the bandit Sandino."

[6, pp. 14–20] I: 380–381.

The Bombing and Siege of El Chipote

(January 1928)

For sixteen days we were under siege, visited daily by the pirate air squadron. . . . The first squadron of four airplanes would arrive at six a.m. and start bombing. Naturally we fired on them, shooting down

---

(October 6, 1927) Sandino declares upcoming elections illegal. *(October 8, 1927)* U.S. airplane shot down and the two pilots executed. Battle of Zaptillal. *(November 1, 1927)* Battle of La Conchita. *(November 6, 1927)* Díaz wins election held under "unofficial" U.S. Marine supervision. *(November 23, 1927)* Marine warplanes locate El Chipote and repeatedly bomb it.

many birds. After four hours of bombing, a new squadron replaced the first and continued the fire for another four hours until another one came. Thus it went successively without stopping until nightfall.

The bombing did us little damage as we were protected, but we lost two hundred head of cattle and the milk cows that fed us. The situation was insupportable due to decomposing dead animals. Buzzards filled the air. . . . Our life became so difficult that we resolved to retreat. We began constructing dummies from straw on which we put hats and left them in the most visible places of El Chipote. Then at night we left. For two more days the aviators bombed the place that was already flattened and vacant. . . . When they arrived we were already a long way away.

[6, pp. 14–20] I: 381–382.

(November 29, 1927) Battle of Las Flores. (December 10, 1927) A Quaker peace delegation arrives. (December 14, 1927) Sandino publishes document suspending the rights of anyone, Nicaraguan or foreign, who aids the foreign intervention.

Kill the Enemy
Wherever and However

(To Froylán Turcios, January 1928)

Dear Maestro:

Defeated in multiple combats in the area
of El Chipote and convinced they were
unable to take our present position, the
yankees used every means possible to im-
pede the arrival of our supplies. They
burned all the valleys and the isolated
houses and corn granaries. They mer-
cilessly killed the inhabitants, of both
sexes and all ages. They totally destroyed
all living animals, leaving the zone deso-
late. Carlton Beals, the journalist, witnessed all this in person. . . .

Today I find myself camped on another
mountain range called El Chipotón, and
since it is not prudent to reveal our plans,
I can only tell our sympathizers not to
worry or be discouraged by our abandon-

*(**December 22, 1927**) Agreement between U.S. and Díaz to officially create the Nicaraguan National Guard.   (**December 30, 1927**) Battles of
Camino Real and Trincheras.*

ment of El Chipote. Our army is very prepared and convinced that our triumph does not consist in holding one position or another but rather in maintaining our armed plan against the invaders. . . .

So that our sympathizers understand the impossibility of our being conquered by the invader, I should tell them that it is much easier for the yankees to overcome a conventional force than Sandino and his columns. . . . Therefore, our mission is to kill the invader wherever and however we can.

If tomorrow or another day it becomes necessary to evacuate this range called El Chipotón [Big Chipote], I have a better range called El Chipotazo [Biggest Chipote].

Patria y Libertad.

[16, 2 p.] I: 229–230.

The Effects of War

(Letter published in El Universal Gráfico, *Mexico, January 19, 1928)*

Our wounded die for lack of prompt medical treatment of their wounds from bombs and shrapnel, just as they die of malaria. I am talking not only of soldiers, but civilians, among whom are many women and children. The enemy airplanes are doing more damage among the population than in our trenches. Ciudad Vieja, Guanacaste, and San Albino have been converted to smoking ruins.

Washington is called the father of the nation; the same is said of Bolívar and Hidalgo. I, alone, am a bandit, according to the standard with which the strong and the weak are measured.

[10, p. 19] I: 224.

Ultimatum from Vice Admiral Sellers

Commander U.S. Special Service Squadron U.S.S. *Rochester* Flagship Managua, Nicaragua, January 20, 1928

General Sandino:

As you know, in accordance with the Stimson Agreement signed last May, the Government of the United States has committed itself to protect the lives and property of American citizens and foreigners, and to conserve order in Nicaragua until the presidential elections are carried out next November.

. . . . Understanding fully the solemn obligation contracted by the United States, to keep order in Nicaragua [by] disarming the inhabitants, my forces have been increased considerably, in men and munitions. We intend to use in full power the vast resources that our Government has put at our disposal.

(January 1, 1928) USMC Lieutenant Bruce killed at Las Cruces. *(January 2, 1928)* U.S. troops attack and burn Quilalí. *(January 4, 1928)* Senator Wheeler of Montana declares that if the Marines want to fight bandits, they should do so in Chicago. *(January 16, 1928)* Sandino sends a message to the Sixth Pan American Conference in Havana, attended by Calvin Coolidge. *(January 26, 1928)* Occupying U.S. forces reach El Chipote, only to find it guarded by straw dummies.

. . . . The unnecessary sacrifice of human lives is so serious that it occurs to me that even though you have refused disarmament on various occasions, now, in the light of subsequent events, you might consider the convenience of putting an end to the present armed resistance to the forces of the United States. I thought you might follow the example of your fellow citizens of both political parties who, last May, came together to resolve their differences with high patriotic spirit, without the further shedding of blood.

Pursuing the policy of my Government to reestablish order expeditiously, I do not feel it justified at this time to restrict any of our energetic military preparations unless you consider it opportune to respond to me immediately, in writing, your willingness to discuss with your companions the ways and means of your acceptance of the Stimson Agreement. It will please me to receive any communication you send,

sent care of the legation of the United States.

D. F. Sellers,
Vice Admiral of the United States Navy, Commander of the Special Service Squadron

> [13, Año 1, No. 569, 1928, p. 58] I: 234–235.

Response to Sellers: Leave Nicaragua

(February 1928)

Mr. D. F. Sellers
Representative of imperialism in Nicaragua

I had formulated a letter in which I answered yours of January 20.

I refer to the final point. Do not think that the origin or basis of this struggle is the

recent revolution. Today the general Nicaraguan population fights to eject the foreign invasion from the country. Regarding the Stimson-Moncada agreements, we have repeated a thousand times that we do not recognize them.

The only way to put an end to this struggle is the immediate withdrawal of invading forces from our territory, the substitution of the actual president by a Nicaraguan citizen who is not candidating for the presidency, and the supervision of the coming elections by Latin American representatives instead of American Marines.

Patria y Libertad,

A. C. Sandino

> [13, Año I, No. 569, 1928, p. 58] I: 233.

(February 1928) The Bishop of Granada blesses the weapons of the Marines as they leave for the Segovias to fight Sandino. (February 3, 1928) Sandino is interviewed in San Rafael del Norte by Carlton Beals of The Nation.

Colonel Salvador Bosque's Fiancée Raped

Colonel Bosque, who distinguished himself as valiant and one of the most daring cavalry riders, conquered the heart of one of the beautiful girls of the Segovias. She was a country girl, but beautiful and cultured. The marriage was to be after the end of the war.

The last battle of the Constitutionalist War was in Teustepe, the first of May, 1927. In this battle Colonel Salvador Bosque died. His fiancée was in mourning and cried incessantly, without consolation. . . .

Then our situation became complicated. Terrible pressure by our enemies obliged me to retreat to the jungles of the Segovias. . . . For more than a year I did not know the names of our unfortunate young girls who were violated by the assassin invader yankees as they passed through defenseless and inoffensive villages.

It was a terrible sensation that I felt when I heard that the young virgin fiancée of the deceased Colonel Bosque had been brutally violated by the miserable yankee invader. As a consequence of that savage act of humiliation, we found her emaciated, astounded, pale, and the mother of a son with blue eyes and ruddy skin who did not know who his father was. What horror! Don't you see that her son is the fruit of the indifference of our Latin American governments in the face of the suffering of my adored and blessed Nicaragua?

[2, pp. 25–27] I: 401–403.

(February 20, 1928) U.S. air attacks on Murra, Nueva Segovia. **(February 27, 1928)** Battle of El Bramadero.

Escalation of Resistance

THE "GUERRILLA" PHASE

March 1928 to January 1929

Sandino's Guerrilla Tactics

I waited in Chipote. The Marines concentrated, shipped up supplies, laid month-long plans to oust me, and crept gradually up and around my position. They are still there. I am here near Jinotega, halfway into the heart of the country. I shall go further into the heart of the country. When they have remobilized here and shipped in troops and more troops and get all set to come out and catch me, I shall be north again, or somewhere else.

[Carlton Beals, "With Sandino in Nicaragua: Send the Bill to Mr. Coolidge," The Nation, Vol. 126, No. 3272 (March 21, 1928) p. 314]

Destruction of La Luz y Los Angeles Mine

8th of May, 1928, El Chipotón

Sr. Froylán Turcios,
Tegucigalpa, Honduras

My very esteemed Maestro:

It was one in the morning of April 29th. The moon was darkened by the smoke of the burning of the four principal buildings of the North American mine La Luz y Los Angeles, in Bluefields Department. The fire was set by orders of this Command.

A note was left to the manager of the company, giving him the reasons that induced us to take this drastic but necessary action.

. . . . Now we have finally comprehended that our worst error would consist of permitting yankee businesses to continue tranquilly exploiting our soil. These enterprises are the basis for the destructive

---

(February 28, 1928) Marine document promotes Sandino from "bandit" to "guerrilla." (March 1928) Sandino moves toward the mining region of the Atlantic Coast. (March 1928) The "Committee for Sandino" is organized in Costa Rica and Mexico. (March 17, 1929) Frank Ross

McCoy is named president of the Nicaraguan National Elections Board by Díaz. (April 3, 1928) U.S. airplanes attack towns of Murra, El Ojoche, El Naranjo, and Quiboto.

and bellicose invasion which they carry out under the pretext of protecting their interests in our country.

[12, Año IV, 1928. p. 1254] I: 262.

No American Safe Here Now

(Note left to Henry Amphlett, La Luz Mine administrator, April 29, 1928)

This mine was destroyed to make tangible our protest against the interventionist war that the USA carries on against Nicaragua. It is a warning that unless the USA recalls the marines, no North American can feel safe in Nicaragua.

For some time I believed that the North American people did not support Calvin Coolidge and his government's abuses in Nicaragua. But I have been convinced in general that the North Americans applaud the Coolidge intervention in my country, and for this reason all North Americans

who fall into my hands will have reached their end.

[10, p. 31] I: 258.

Sandino Interprets the Monroe Doctrine

(To Froylán Turcios, June 10, 1928)

The yankees are the worst enemy of our people. When they see us in moments of patriotic inspiration, sincerely seeking unification, they stir up our deep-seated pending differences, inciting hate among us so that we continue disunited and weak. We are consequently easy to colonize.

We are fully into the twentieth century and the time has come to prove to the whole world that the yankees have distorted their own theme. Speaking of the Monroe Doctrine they say: *America for the Americans.* Now that is well said. All of us who are born in America are Americans. The mistake that the imperialists have made is that they have interpreted the Monroe Doctrine thus: *America for the yankees.* Now then, so that the blond idiots do not continue to be fooled, I reform the phrase in the following terms: *The United States of America for the yankees. Latin America for the Indio-Latins.*

[10, pp. 27–28] I: 270–272.

Appeal to Latin American Solidarity

El Chipotón, August 4, 1928

Gentlemen Presidents:

Being in the interests of the fifteen nations that will be most affected if the yankees make Nicaragua a colony of Uncle Sam, I address you with the rude frankness of a soldier, not with hypocritical and false diplomatic courtesies.

The yankees, with some discretion, wish to disguise themselves on a project to construct an interoceanic canal through Nicaraguan territory, which will result in isolation between Indio-Hispanic republics. . . . Do the Latin American governments really think that the yankees only want to conquer Nicaragua and then they will be satisfied? Have you perhaps forgotten that six of the twenty-one republics of America have lost their sovereignty? Panama, Puerto Rico, Cuba, Haiti, Santo Domingo, and Nicaragua have become colonies of yankee imperialism. These governments do not defend the collective interest of their citizens, because they came to power not by popular will, but rather by imposition of imperialism. . . .

Perhaps the Ibero-American governments haven't understood that the yankees make fun of their self-serving politics adopted in cases like Nicaragua. . . . If they had more consciousness of their historical responsibility they would not wait

(April 16, 1928) The U.S. Senate Foreign Relations Committee orders an investigation regarding Marine operations in Nicaragua. The Senate questions the authority of the President to send and maintain troops in Nicaragua. (April 1928) Support for Sandino is voiced by the Sixth World Congress of the Comintern in Moscow. (April 29, 1928) A North American gold mine is taken.

until conquest ravages their own soils. They would come to the defense of a brother republic that fights with valor and tenacity born of desperation against an enemy a hundred times larger and armed with modern weaponry. . . .

We are ninety million Hispano-Americans and we need only to unite. . . . The worthy people of Latin America should imitate Bolívar, Hidalgo, San Martín, and the Mexican children who, on September 13, 1847, fell riddled by yankee bullets in Chapultepec. They died in defense of the Homeland and the Race rather than submit to a life of shame under yankee imperialism.

Patria y Libertad.

Augusto C. Sandino

[10, pp. 34–38] I: 276–279.

Jungle War Takes Toll on Invaders

(Río Coco, August 10, 1928)

Our guns have been covered with glory upon completely exterminating a column of 150 Marines. They came up the Río Coco trying to reach our defended position. . . . The combat lasted for several hours. The Marines disembarked and we fought them, killing 78 and wounding 28. Finally we sank their boats, drowning the crew and the survivors of combat.

The 28 wounded we had captured also died, consequence of an epidemic among them, which here is known as "remoral." Only our men, accustomed to life in these inhospitable regions, were saved from this disease.

[16, 1 p.] I: 280.

Sandino Rejects
Election of Moncada

November 20, 1928

My dear Maestro Turcios:

I have the honor of letting you know that I have taken the step of inviting the Liberal Republican and Liberal parties and the Solidarity Group to unify their action with our army. This is the result of the yankee intervention in the presidential elections of the 4th of this month, in which they imposed the traitor José María Moncada as president.

. . . . I don't need to tell you that if the buccaneers do not withdraw and if the unification does not materialize, I will continue with my army combating the invaders and the traitors to the Homeland.

And, again, if for whatever reason the army does not respond to the call I make to them, I will remain all alone, taking it

---

(May 13, 1928) USMC Capt. Hunter killed at La Flor and Capt. Williamson at El Zapote. (June 22, 1928) Salvadoran militant Farabundo Martí joins the Sandinista Army and becomes member of Supreme Command (August 15). (August 7, 1928) Battle of Río Coco, Segovias. (November 6, 1928) Under Marine supervision, José María Moncada is elected president of Nicaragua.

to the buccaneers one shot here and one shot there, without mercy. God is with us in this. He will take us to the definitive triumph.

[11, pp. 109–110] I: 287–288.

Reply to Admiral Sellers's Appeal

El Chipotón, Nicaragua, January 1, 1929

Mr. D. F. Sellers
Rear Admiral U.S. Navy,
Corinto, Nicaragua

Sir:

Your communication is at hand, signed the 4th of December last year, in which, despite earlier failures to communicate peacefully with me, you appeal once more to my patriotism to stop the armed resistance. At the petition of the usurper Días, you are trying to restore order to the whole country.

The patriotism to which you appeal is what has been maintaining me to repel force with force, while absolutely not accepting any intervention by your government in the internal affairs of our nation. A nation's sovereignty is not discussed, but rather defended with weapons in hand. This same sentiment moves me today to manifest to you that only with General José M. Moncada could I enter into an agreement to bring about an effective peace in our country.

As a member of the Liberal Party, which he betrayed, he can rectify his errors through a commitment entered upon with us, with the Nicaraguan people, and with the Liberal Party, to respect the basis [for peace] which will be proposed soon by our Liberating Army. To arrive at an effective peace accord with General José M. Moncada, we establish as the first absolutely indispensable principle the withdrawal of the North American forces under your command from our territory.

Without these conditions, *there will be no peace*. Even though your communiqué said that there is no purpose to my continued armed resistance, I declare that only the continuation of my armed resistance will bring the benefits to which you allude.

I don't think it is too much to say that the lives and properties of foreigners will be better guaranteed by us, the Nicaraguans, than by forces of a foreign government. Intromission into our affairs will only bring loss of peace and the wrath of the people.

Patria y Libertad.

A. C. Sandino

[11, pp. 118–119; 16, 2 p.] I: 291–293.

(November 27, 1928) U.S. president-elect Herbert Hoover visits Nicaragua and holds talks aboard ship with Moncada, Díaz, and Emiliano Chamorro. (December 6, 1928) At El Cuje, U.S. Marines fight their last official battle in Nicaragua as responsibility shifts from them to the Nicaraguan National Guard, led by U.S. Marine officers. (December 28, 1928) Froylán Turcios resigns as Representative of Sandino's Army in the exterior.

Basis for a Treaty to Constitutionalize the Election of José M. Moncada

(January 6, 1929)

1. Demand the immediate withdrawal of U.S. invading forces from our territory.
2. Reject any yankee loan, and seek any loans from Nicaraguan capitalists.
3. Consider null the Chamorro-Bryan Treaties, which diminish sovereignty.
4. Reject vigorously any U.S. intervention in our internal affairs.
5. Recognize the newly delineated territory we call San Juan de Segovia.
6. Declare free the cultivation and trade of tobacco in the Republic.
7. A maximum of eight hours work per day in industrial or agricultural enterprises, of national or foreign owners. Over eight hours will be overtime.
8. All enterprises must pay worker wages in cash, not coupons, script, or other forms now used. Pay shall be made every ten days.
9. All enterprises which employ more than fifteen operators or families must maintain, at their costs, schools for the primary education of workers of both sexes.
10. Women must be given the same salary as men, for equal work executed, and their work adjusted according to their physical conditions.
11. Children's work shall be regulated so they can attend school, and they must work in moral and hygienic conditions.
12. The right to organize workers of both sexes into unions must be established. Congress shall recognize the right to strike of all worker organizations.
13. Nicaragua should not pay any of the military costs incurred by the U.S. resulting from its invasion of our territory.
14. The Government must deal with the matter of the unity of Central America.
15. The Government must give the greatest guarantees to the peasants in general, [particularly] to those of the Dept. of Nueva Segovia, Jinotega, Estelí, and Matagalpa, since they have made common cause with our Army.

[16, 5 p.] I: 297–303.

Internationalization of the Struggle

January 1929 to May 1930

Sandino Refutes Misinformation

(February 24, 1929)

The news has come to our Camp that, unsurprisingly, General José María Moncada has lied in a most miserable way, saying that we have proposed the division of Nicaragua into two sections: one governed by me and the other by him. Nobody believes this. My fervent desire to unify morally and materially not only Central America but also Latin America and the Antilles is well known to the civilized world. Therefore, I could not think of dividing Nicaragua. And even though this attitude is well known to the outside world, it is useful to make these declarations so that it will become known in Nicaragua. Nicaragua's corrupt press covers up what is happening in our own country.

The yankees make Moncada attribute to me ideas I could never conceive of in order to give them a pretext to stay in Nicaragua. They consider me a small enemy and not once have they understood that in this land, in which many lick their feet, there are also those who spit on them.

[16, 3 p.] I: 318–320.

To President Hoover on Failed Policy

(March 6, 1929)

Mr. Hoover:

If you have eyes to see, look. If you have ears to hear, listen. Coolidge and Kellogg are a pair of failed politicians. Their action in Nicaragua has sunk the land of Washington to the lowest depths of discredit. They have caused the shedding of blood and torrents of tears in my Homeland. They have also plunged many North American homes into mourning and caused weeping.

You have only a tiny group of immoral friends in Nicaragua, who do not represent the sentiments of the Nicaraguan people. I represent, with my Army, the true sentiments of our citizens. The great majority of Nicaraguans is with me.

I am aware of the material resources which your country has. You have everything, but "you are lacking God." If you continue the politics of Coolidge and Kellogg, you will continue to find Sandinos.

[16, 4 p.] I: 324–328.

Appeal to Central American Presidents

El Chipotón, Nicaragua, C. A.
March 12, 1929

Dear Sirs:

In the desire to free my Homeland, I have sought to represent myself before the four

---

(1929) The crash of the New York stock market and economic depression are felt worldwide. (January 8, 1929) Moncada enlists paramilitary "Volunteers" outside the National Guard to act against Sandino's sympathizers. (January 18, 1929) Battles of Guanacaste and San Antonio result in high Marine losses. (January 20, 1929) Herbert Hoover inaugurated and Stimson becomes Secretary of State.

governments that still remain in Central America.

Unable to go in person, I send a symbol. Enclosed is a leaf from the Segovian jungles, where the Honor of Nicaragua is being defended. The name of the tree of this leaf is *palanca*.

In these moments Nicaragua has a lever [*palanca*] like Archimedes had and we need a point of support equal to the one he sought. I beg of you to consult your people to see if there you find the support that this part of the Greater Homeland [Central America] seeks through me. Archimedes could move the earth. We, together, can avoid being humiliated by the yankee. If Nicaragua doesn't find the support that it seeks in its brother republics, perhaps this note will find its place in history.

[16, 1 p.] I: 332.

Proposal to Latin American Presidents on the Nicaraguan Canal Project

(March 20, 1929)

The interoceanic canal of Nicaragua should be opened . . . but this opening cannot be resolved by Nicaragua and the United States alone. A project of this nature transcends our interests. It is for the inhabitants of all the earth.

To carry out this project it is necessary to consult with all of Latin America. . . . Already a mistake was made by failing to consult our Indio-Hispanic America about the opening of the Panama Canal. But we can still avoid another error.

If we permit the United States to open a canal in Nicaragua, without any commitment on its part to respect the sovereignty and independence of our nations, we would commit a wrong, even to the

United States of North America. They would feel even stronger than God and would defy all the world, which would bring as consequence the destruction of their own great nation.

[16, 2 p.] I: 338–340.

U.S. Colonial Power and Arrogance

(Declaration, October 1929)

We have said many times that the North Americans consider it necessary to colonize Nicaragua in order to be able to construct an interoceanic canal across its territory and establish a naval base in the Gulf of Fonseca. Both require North American financing.

This is a demonstration of how nations arrive at an apogee of power which they cannot maintain because, arriving at this point, they become arrogant. This arrogance leads to their fall. It is not hidden

---

(February 3, 1929) Martial law is declared. (May 24, 1929) Sandino leaves for Mexico to seek support. (June 15, 1929) The United States asks Moncada to disband his paramilitary "Volunteer" units. (June 28, 1929) Sandino arrives at the port of Veracruz and stays in Mérida, Yuca- *tán, supported by 1,000 pesos a month from President Portes Gil. (July 22–24, 1929) Sandino's representative to the Second World Anti-Imperialist League meeting in Frankfort gains support for his cause.*

from anyone that the United States has reached the maximum of its development; for this reason it does not respect the rights of others. But at this moment the finger of justice is about to mark its noisy collapse.

Our Army is showing that while there are miserable politicians who lick the feet of the invader, there are also honorable and patriotic men who have known and will know how to defend, with gun in hand, the integrity of the territory that our fore-fathers left us.

[2, pp. 7–9] I: 399.

Isolation Drives Sandino to Mexico

(*Interview with* El Dictamen, *Veracruz, Mexico, October 1929*)

We need, not arms, not money, not bullets, but rather the moral support, the sympathy which we have always had with all the peoples of America. The silence, the isolation afflict us—the desperation of remaining ignored. We needed the world to know that we were still in the struggle. For this reason I left Nicaragua.

The resignation of Froylán Turcios resulted in isolation. When he was our representative in Honduras we were in communication with the world. . . . Our cause has gotten weaker abroad for lack of communication and lack of the spiritual interchange which encourages us in the struggle. Now I have found our representative, Dr. Pedro José Zepeda, in whom we have absolute confidence. He will do what we need. Tranquil now in this regard, we return to the fight. Naturally the struggle has not ceased. I stand in the breach even outside Nicaragua.

[11, pp. 135–137] I: 392–394.

Mexico Yields to Pressure and Denies Aid

Mérida, Mexico. December 4, 1929

Most excellent Mr. President of the United States of Mexico:

May I invite you to manifest your final decision regarding Mexico's response to our actual circumstances. . . . Our leaving the Segovias to come to Mexico has been life and death for supporting the cause of Nicaraguan national sovereignty. However, until now, Mr. President, I have not seen the slightest indication that the needs that brought me to Mexico can be fulfilled.

I find myself very pensive since I have understood that you covertly deny me a personal interview. I am aware of the consequences for Mexico if you interview me, but neither do I ignore how Mexico has been wise. She will know how to maintain herself in the face of the insolent pre-

(September 27, 1929) In Nicaragua, Sandinista Gen. Pedro Altamirano leads attack against La Colonia. (October 1929) Sandino gives interview to El Dictamen *of Veracruz. (January 12, 1930) Battle of Buena Vista. (January 27, 1930) In Mexico City, Sandino gives interviews to* New York World *and* El Universal. *(January 29, 1930) Sandino meets with Mexican President Portes Gil. (February 17, 1930) Sandino sends message to the 7th National Mexican Student Congress in Monterrey.*

tensions of the United States of North America to colonize Central America.

A. C. Sandino

[17, 4 p.] I: 404–407.

Sandino's Humanity and Mission

January 2, 1930

My very appreciated brother Altamirano:

I send you four boxes of 38 Special cartridges and two 38 Smith and Wessons, for your faithful followers.

Keep before you and all the other brothers in this struggle that I am nothing more than a simple instrument of divine justice to redeem this nation. If I need anything of this world's miserable goods it is because I was born also of woman. I came to you full of the same human needs as all of us who live on this terrestrial ball. I was one of you and spoke like you, otherwise you would not have believed in me.

Remember always, General Altamirano, that I esteem you sincerely, you and all those who have been with me from the beginning.

Patria y Libertad.

[11, pp. 147–148] II: 40.

Response to Press Reports that He Sold Out for $60,000

(January 8, 1930)

We read in the clippings sent from *La Prensa* and *The New York Times*, both of December 26 last year, as well as some newspapers from Central America, the news that we were offered $60,000 to leave the Segovias.

We believe that this allegation is the vile work of yankee agents. The form of this slander indicates that its author does not know anything about our integrity of

character, nor that Sandino and his men come entirely from the working and peasant class. We never crawl to get soft paying jobs at the expense of the blood of martyrs in the struggle to liberate the oppressed.

This calumny to besmirch free men's honor is the work of impotent, worthless parasites, unscrupulous fakes, unable to put their lives on the altar of a noble cause. They do not even have sufficient moral courage to sign their names to their allegations.

[16, 2 p.] II: 41–42.

Reply to a Questionnaire from *El Universal* of Mexico

(January 28, 1930)

"It is said that you had decided to abandon your liberation of Nicaragua and that you are going to the United States. How true is this?"

(March 3, 1930) Sandino returns to Mérida, Yucatán, from Mexico City and prepares to return to Nicaragua. (April 1, 1930) Attack on the National Guard headquarters in Yalí, Nicaragua. The Military Academy is inaugurated in Managua, directed by U.S. military officials. (April 4,

1930) U.S. Ambassador Matthew E. Hanna assumes post in Managua.

If our intention were to abandon the fight in Nicaragua, we would not have chosen Mexico, because Mexico is a country hospitable to free men and revolutionaries, never to those who back down on principles or fail. The United States has always been the favorite attraction of the Judases.

"What is the situation in your country?"

At this moment our struggle is to conserve our war elements until we renew our activities. . . . The Nicaraguan politicians have created an unprecedented situation of servitude to the United States. . . . We consider the yankees as enemies, and when they fall in our hands, they receive what we call the "cut of the vest"—automatic decapitation.

[16, 2 p.] II: 59–61.

The Futility of Fighting False Rumors

Mérida, Yucatán, 3rd of March, 1930

Sr. Victor Manuel Palomo
Director of *Renovación Obrera*
Guatemala

Dear Sir:

The cunning procedure of our enemies should not surprise sympathizers of our Cause, since the weapons they believe strongest to attack us are calumny and defamation.

Now we must not waste time attacking falsehoods and clarifying the black storm clouds that they launch. The grave responsibility on our shoulders, on the shoulders of all conscious men in Latin America, shows us the urgency of not losing time in "plowing the ocean," as the Liberator [Bolívar] said. Our energies must be concentrated toward one goal only, that of saving the dignity of our nations from shipwreck. They are threatened by villainy from within and voracity from without.

[16, 3 p.] II: 79–80.

(April 11, 1930) Augustín Farabundo Martí leaves Sandino and returns to El Salvador to take up liberation struggle there. (April 19, 1930) The International Acceptance Bank of New York becomes the new financial agent of Nicaragua. (April 24, 1930) Sandino secretly leaves Mexico for Nicaragua. He arrives in the Segovian mountains on May 16. (May 8, 1930) Hoover names USMC Captain Alfred W. Johnson as president of the Nicaraguan National Electoral Committee.

War and Resistance Intensify

June 1930 to September 1931

Return to the Segovias
to Continue the Struggle

(To Estéban Pavletich in Mexican jail)

Mérida, Yucatán, March 30, 1930

In these days we return to the Segovias with hands empty and conscience clean, even though our enemies have tried to crucify us on the cross of calumny, as you know. We will overcome every obstacle and arrive at our beloved camps of battle to give new proof of our love for Latin America by our dignified resistance to the invader. We repeat the phrases of Bolívar: *If the elements are against us, we will be against the elements; and if God is against us, we will be against God.* If God is just, he will be on our side.

I will not again leave the Segovian battlefield, not even dead, while one miserable yankee invader exists on Nicaraguan soil. . . .

I lament not to be able to offer you any financial help. In our coffers we have a few cents only.

[16, 3 p.] II: 114.

Sandino Wounded
in Battle of Saraguazca

To the Honorable Press of the Entire World. June 19, 1930.

On the night of the 19th, I was informed that some suspicious lights descended from El Saraguazca, in the heights of El Chirinagua, as if to approach our front lines.

A cold breeze was whipping the heights, as usual. No doubt remained that the lights we saw were of the enemy. In the fog, General Pedro Altamirano arrived with ten men on horseback, bringing similar news about the approaching enemy.

Three mortar shots were ordered as an immediate sign to all our outposts that covered El Saraguazca.

The combat started in the first hours of the 19th at San Marcos. At twelve noon, the enemy had been defeated on all flanks. The yankee commander died on the first assault.

The enemy renewed fire almost without letup until six that evening. Our brave soldiers' fire completely annihilated them.

A fleet of six airplanes bombed and machine-gunned us twice with fury.

It was a terrible day for the yankees and for the renegade Nicaraguans.

In that tragic moment of our history, strange and impressive scenes were recorded. The enemy losses were innumerable, as well as the number of deserters.

On our part we had to lament the death of Captain Encarnación Lumbí, and the wounding of young soldier Roque Matey, of Telpaneca.

(June 1, 1930) *Detention camps are set up for people suspected of aiding Sandino. Whole villages are evacuated.* *(June 6 to August 29, 1930)* *Sandinista forces engage the enemy in fourteen battles throughout the central and northern provinces. U.S. air bombardments increase in intensity.* *Sandino is wounded in his left leg in air attack.* *(July 9, 1930)* *Twelve hundred new recruits join Sandino's army in El Saraguazca region.* *(September 1930)* *The Nicaraguan National Guard is reorganized, putting political leaders and judges under its authority.*

As the air bombing was about to cease, at four in the afternoon, an enemy bomb exploded, and one of the shrapnel fragments wounded slightly my left leg.

. . . . Four hours later we occupied the heights of El Saraguazca according to plan. Thus ended that armed action in which two races disputed, the one for supremacy, and the other for the right of Homeland and Liberty.

[16, 3 p.] II: 117–121.

Founding of the National Guard

To the World Press, June 19, 1930.

The North American piracy has been able to organize an army of Nicaraguan youth which it calls the National Guard. . . .

Is it possible that a military uniform, three scant meals a day, and twelve pesos a month which these men receive would make them live so happily that they are

(October 1, 1930) The combined USMC and Nicaraguan National Guard troops number 5,000. *(November 12, 1930) The Foreign Policy Association reports the starvation of two hundred people, including women and children, in detention camps in northern Nicaragua.*

able to forget the beloved Motherland that kisses us all under the same blue sky?

Who is really responsible for so much infamy? José María Moncada, Adolfo Díaz, and Emiliano Chamorro! O, what a cursed trinity of miserable traitors!

It doesn't matter that traitors have multiplied in Nicaragua. Our Army is fully imbued with its high historical role to sweep this social putrefaction out with the brooms of our bayonets.

Patria y Libertad.

[16, 3 p.] II: 117–121.

Disavowal of Communist Party Affiliation

August 15, 1930

Sr. Dr. Pedro José Zepeda,
Representative of our Army,
Mexico City

(November 19, 1930) Sandinista attack spreads south to Telica, León. (December 8, 1930) National Guard soldiers revolt against their authorities in Somoto, Madriz. (January 2, 1931) Senator William Borah of Idaho calls for the immediate evacuation of U.S. troops from Nicaragua.

For me it is difficult to enter into discussions with stupid people like those who have attacked me behind my back when I am fully engaged in major activities against our common enemy and unable to defend myself against new slander.

. . . . In what way, could I be traitor to a party to which I have never belonged?

We have had correspondence with all the anti-imperialist groups of the Continent, but with none have we had political commitments, because our own Army regulations prohibit it.

Where then is the betrayal of the Communist Party?

Patria y Libertad.

[16, 3 p.] II: 133–134.

Military Operations During August, 1930

Recent battles by our Army against the mercenary forces:

The forces of General Pedro Antonio Irías and Miguel Angel Ortez heroically engaged the enemy in Independencia, Jinotega, the 18th of August. The enemy lost more than sixty lives. We lost fifteen, because we held the best positions.

On the 19th of the same month, in Soledad, the enemy was able to defeat our forces after a fierce battle. We lost some munitions and some cavalry supply mules.

On the 21st of August, in El Bálsamo, there was an encounter between the family of General Pedro Altamirano and the enemy. The gunfire was short but bloody. The oldest son of General Altamirano, named Encarnación, died in the fray. Also a little girl and General Altamirano's daughter-in-law were wounded, as well

as three other children of his, Victorina, Melecio, and Pedro, Jr. The enemy lost seven men on the battlefield.

On the 21st, the forces of Colonel Perfecto Charvarría launched an ambush in Pavona, taking many provisions and medicine from the enemy.

On the 23rd, the forces of Colonel Fulgencio Hernández Báez sprang an ambush at Río Ducalí. Three yankees and five turncoat National Guards died, and twenty-five enemy were wounded. Our forces took jackets, cloaks, and medicines.

On the 28th, at nine in the morning, sporadic shooting across the river began, got formidably louder at three p.m., and lasted until the sunset painted the sky. At five a.m. on the 29th the bloody combat began again. . . . There were more than one hundred losses on their side and ours. We captured a box of books in English, twelve boxes of large cannon missiles. . . .

(February 6, 1931) Col. Calvin B. Matthew becomes head of the Nicaraguan National Guard.

(March 31, 1931) The city of Managua is destroyed by a powerful earthquake. U.S. Marines patrol the city. Col. Matthew declares martial law.

There have been eight more lesser battles after this bloody combat, among which San Rafael del Norte stands out, led by General Pedro Blandón.

Patria y Libertad.

[16, 2 p.] II: 142–144.

On Love, Justice, and Peace

October 14, 1930

Sr. Colonel Abraham Rivera,
Río Coco, Segovias

Be always ready, dear brother Rivera, to defend just causes, even though you undergo every sacrifice imaginable, because sacrifice is *love (the creator, or God)*.

Injustice comes from not knowing the divine laws . . . and for this, injustice cannot stand because it is against the law of *love*. Love is the only law that will reign on earth when brotherhood arrives and men are of the *light,* as the Father Creator commands.

To destroy injustice it has been necessary to attack it, and we have seen many come with this mission on earth, among whom is Jesus. Everyone who fights for people's freedom continues his doctrines. . . .

The earth produces everything necessary for the happiness and comfort of the human genus, but for long millions of centuries injustice has reigned over the earth and the existence of everything necessary for humans has been in the hands of a few big shots. The great majority of people lack even the indispensable. Some die from hunger after producing with their sweat what others squander on binges.

But there will be justice. The war of the Liberators will destroy the oppressors, after which justice and a resulting peace will come on earth.

Dear brother Colonel Rivera, don't be bored by my explanations in this letter. I have noted in you much intelligence. And I am interested that the men who surround me be saturated by the greatest love of justice, because she is our standard of liberty.

Patria y Libertad.

[11, pp. 175–177] II: 145–147.

Appropriating Commerce in the War Zone

Orders to all Commanders,
October 16, 1930

Very appreciated brothers:

The inhabitants of all the countryside where we operate live in desperation for salt and medicines. They risk their lives to get these in villages where the enemy mercenaries are holed up. Knowing that salt and medicines are brought by traders who defy our operations, you are to au-

---

(April 11, 1931) Sandino forces attack and destroy installations of the United Fruit Company on the Atlantic Coast. General Blandón dies in air attack at Logtown (April 13). (April 15, 1931) Sandino forces occupy Cabo Gracias a Dios on the Atlantic. U.S. warships arrive at Puerto Cabezas and Marines disembark. The USS Rochester *patrols the coast at Bluefields. (May 30, 1931) USMC Col. Julian C. Smith declares martial law in the departments of Matagalpa and Jinotega.*

thorize all the neighbors of the country-side to denounce whatever shipment of merchandise goes through one town to another. Our forces will confiscate any shipment and distribute it to the closest neighbors.

The troop will take only what is necessary for its consumption at the moment, and will continue its march.

If anyone refuses to give up his shipment, that man will be put in front of the guns.

The motive for ordering execution is the following: The traders who work around here are accomplices of the yankee invader in the sacking and assassination of our people, without regard to our Army. Because they are accomplices, we must make them feel with more force the rigor of justice in defense of the Nation.

Whoever doesn't want to receive the goods that our Army confiscates from the traitors of the Homeland should be considered future traitors and for this reason must be executed.

Patria y Libertad.

[11, pp. 177–178] II: 148–149.

Managua Earthquake Adds to Suffering

(March 31, 1931)

As a human and, above all, as a Nicaraguan, I am filled with consternation by the disaster. I don't know if this is destiny, but no people have suffered so much in history from the injustice of men: the cruel U.S. military occupation; the pretexts to maintain our territory under the iron boot of intervention; the evil sons who traffic with the blood of the people and with the Nation's honor; the rape of the public economy by "protectors" who control our banks, our customs houses, our railroads; the systematic assassination of all honorable men who do not accept such things; and, on top of everything else, the orchestrated slander to call us common "bandits."

If the earthquake is an aid from Providence to prevent the dismembering of our territory, God must take into account the blood of so many victims, and unite it with the blood already spilt of hundreds of men sacrificed in the Segovias. May it maintain a flame in the symbolic lamp of world liberty.

[16, 2 p.] II: 167.

(June 18, 1931) President Moncada solicits U.S. supervision of the upcoming elections. (July–September 1931) Sandino's columns deploy throughout Nicaragua and engage in battles: La Libertad, Chontales (July 12), Puerto Waspuck, Zelaya (July 17), Ciudad Rama, Siquia (July 21), Río Coco (July 22), La Pavona (July 24), and Acoyapa, Chontales (September 3). An American airplane is downed in Sacklin. Sandino controls four-fifths of the Nicaraguan territory.

Manifesto on Hoover and U.S. Prestige

(May 1931)

Like an impotent furious beast, the yankee president, Herbert Clark Hoover, throws himself into insults against the commander of the Army that is liberating Nicaragua. He and Stimson are modern assassins, as were Coolidge and Kellogg. The North American people can thank this quartet for all policy failures. The fathers, sons, and brothers of the Marines who have fallen in the Segovian battlefields curse now and forever these disastrous governors.

The insolent blustering of Coolidge in 1927, saying that he would forcibly disarm our Army, has a high cost to the prestige of the United States. Lately we have learned that Herbert Clark Hoover, who will not be reelected in 1932, has prom-

(September 24, 1931) USMC commander, Gen. Ben H. Fuller, arrives in Nicaragua and is met at Corinto by Anastasio Somoza García, Under-Secretary of Foreign Relations. *(October 27, 1931)* American logging company centers of Logtown and Luisiana are taken. *(November 1,* 1931) Municipal elections supervised by U.S. Marines. *(November 23, 1931)* Managuans panic as Sandinista forces attack Chichigalpa, 120 kilometers from the capital.

91

ised that he will capture Sandino to deliver him to justice. This is verbal compensation for the beating our Army has just given the yankees on the Atlantic Coast, leaving Logtown strewn with their cadavers. We are not to blame. We only defend ourselves.

[10, pp. 132–133] II: 179.

Sandino's Success Against All Odds

(Manifesto, July 28, 1931)

Our Army combats an army provided with very modern war equipment and every other material resource that its government has. Nevertheless, we have controlled the countryside in eight departments of Nicaragua. We haven't taken cities because this is not yet in our program, but we will do it when the time comes. Our tactic consists of maintaining the towns and cities surrounded in the provinces where we operate. . . .

Our Army is the most disciplined, self-denied, and disinterested of all the earth, because it is conscious of its high historical role. It does not matter that false stories classify us as "bandits." Time and history will tell if the bandits are in the Nicaraguan Segovias, where love and human brotherhood reign. Even in the cases where our Army orders the execution of traitors, this is done for the highest love of liberty.

[1, pp. 109–111, 114] I: 186–188.

Attack Alone with Your Pistol if Necessary

Sr. General Francisco Estrada,
Military Operations Camp

My dear brother:

According to your note of October 27, your men are all together with you. . . .

March urgently on the town of Quilalí and attack the sentry-boxes, seeking triumph even though you use up all your ammunition. General Díaz has received all the munition stores and will not delay in reaching you once the enemy has pulled back from the mountain.

If your men are afraid to attack, you will go out alone with your pistol and fire upon the town. There are no more instructions for the moment.

An embrace for all.

Patria y Libertad.

A. C. Sandino

[11, p. 277] II: 204.

(November 25, 1931) The U.S. Embassy reports that the situation in Nicaragua is worse than ever as Sandino's troops consecutively attack Mayacundo, Santa Isabelia, and Valle de Las Zapatas in León province. (December 10, 1931) U.S. Congress is informed by an investigative committee that Nicaragua is the best route for a new isthmus canal. President Hoover reiterates his intention to bring the Marines home. (December 22, 1931) Sandinista column occupies San Isidro, Matagalpa.

Year of Negotiation

SANDINO IS A POLITICAL FORCE

1932

Differences with Farabundo Martí, Salvadoran Martyr

(Related to Nicolás Arrieta in Niquinohomo, November 1933)

"What do you say, General, of your differences with Farabundo Martí?"

I conversed many times with Farabundo on political and social questions. He insisted on transforming my struggle into a struggle for socialism. I agreed with all his ideas and admired his talent, his sincerity, but I explained to him that for the moment this was not possible and that my fight had to continue as a nationalist and anti-imperialist struggle.

I explained that the primary task was to defend the Nicaraguan nation against imperialist clutches, free her from this, throwing these dogs and the yankee companies off our soil, and that the next step to take was to organize the laborers. His enthusiasm and good faith impressed me vividly and I greatly lamented his death.

[17, 21 p.] II: 366.

To Stop the Machiavellian Elections

(To civilian authorities in Jinotega, Matagalpa, and Estelí, August 31, 1932)

Now as before, we are convinced that no government of Nicaragua arising from foreign vigilance will seek our interests. To the contrary, they will protect even more the foreigners who illegally put them in power. Sufficient reason that no one worthy of being Nicaraguan should show up at the Machiavellian elections that the enemy prepares for the months of October and November of this year.

[2, pp. 61–62] II: 246–247.

(January 4, 1932) U.S. government sends Admiral Clark H. Woodward to head the National Election Board of Nicaragua. Nicaragua's Supreme Court ratifies him. *(February 1–19, 1932)Farabundo Martí is executed in El Salvador (February 1) after his peasant army of 3,000 is massacred.*

In Nicaragua, battles intensify: Peña Blanca (February 1), Biltiguí (February 2), San Antonio (February 14), Poza Honda (February 24), and El Sauce (February 27). U.S. Marines level houses and arrest 20 citizens in Managua (February 19).

Sabotage Communications and Harass

On the 7th of this month, our Supreme Command issued a decree, ordering the destruction of telephone and telegraph lines in order to interrupt the elections that the invading power pretends to verify. Harassment of the enemy, in every form, must intensify from now until January first.

(signed) F. Estrada, Staff Chief

[10, p. 177] II: 247–248.

Contingency Plans for Peace When U.S. Troops Leave After Elections

La Chispa, November 9, 1932.

My dearly beloved brother Altamirano:

The elections are over and now we are waiting to know if it is Sacasa or the

---

(March 1, 1932) Franklin Roosevelt inaugurated as president of the United States. (April 1932) Nicaraguan National Guardsmen revolt in Kisalaya and Quilalí. Some of these join Sandino.

Conservatives against whom we are going to continue fighting, because the pirates will leave January second.

Currently I am busy elaborating the basis for a treaty which we will present to Sacasa, if it is he who is elected.

On the other hand, if the Conservatives stay in power, I believe that neither they nor we will seek an agreement. I think we will resolve the matter at gunpoint.

[11, pp. 372–374] II: 249–251.

U.S. War Planes Leave Nicaragua but Hostilities Continue

(Letter to General Pedro Altamirano, December 18, 1932)

There are now no warplanes in Nicaragua. They left on a ship on the 15th of this month. Only commercial airlines which carry no machine guns or bombs cross our airspace. I have been so notified by the loyal Sofonías Salvatierra. For this reason, we no longer have to harass airplanes and all our precautions will be with the enemy on land. These dogs do not want to die but they will not want to attack us. The most they will do is defend their positions until we have arrived at a practical understanding.

. . . . We have said that our hostilities will not stop without arriving at an effective agreement, and only then will we suspend orders to attack. As for me, I feel that it will be better if we can take some towns beforehand, because the enemy will thus understand more precisely the need for a treaty.

[11, pp. 384–385] II: 261.

(April 15 to May 18, 1932) Sandino forces press attacks in Ocotal (April 15 and 21), Kisalaya (April 21), Bellorín and Ciudad Antigua (May 1), Mos in Atlantic Coast (May 16), and Achuapa, León (May 18). (May 22, 1932) Yankee planes bomb Sandinista positions around the Neptune mine, Zelaya, and the U.S. announces the sending of more troops to Nicaragua. (June 1932) Liberal presidential candidate Juan B. Sacasa asks Washington for the continued presence of the Marines in Nicaragua.

On Commission for a Peaceful Solution

December 24, 1932

Sr. Sofonías Salvatierra.

Very distinguished sir:

We take this happy opportunity to send you our highest congratulations for your work in favor of the restoration of our national independence. . . . We have no reservations in receiving the peace commission. . . .

Dr. Sacasa should take the opportunity presented to him for an agreement with our Army, so he does not continue as a straw-man puppet. His last time as president he remained as the toy of the little boys. We have power over Dr. Sacasa, because he abandoned us in decisive moments of our national history. As a private individual, the doctor merits our appreciation, but as a public man, it is our respon-

---

(June 30, 1932) National Guardsmen mutiny at the San Isidro garrison in Matagalpa. (July 5, 1932) The U.S. Vaccaro Banana Company near Puerto Cabezas is taken. U.S. troops penetrate Nicaragua from Honduras.

sibility to point out his past to him. . . .

My wife, my brother Sócrates, and I send you and your distinguished family our fraternal embrace.

[8, pp. 105–107] II: 262–263.

Sandino's Army Designates Representatives to Proposed Peace Talks

December 24, 1932

To the distinguished:
    don Salvador Calderón Ramírez,
    Doctor Escolástico Lara,
    Doctor Pedro José Zepeda, and
    General Horacio Portocarrero.

Our Army considers you the most illustrious sons of Nicaragua because your public acts have always been in line with the highest spirit of patriotism. . . .

Today we have been informed that the Nicaraguan people, awakened to patriotism by the sounds of our liberating weapons, are unanimously interested in a patriotic accord to be made between Dr. Sacasa and our Army. If the government of Sacasa is independent, without public or private commitments to the United States, we are resolved to carry out a peace conference in the town of San Rafael del Norte.

We designate you to represent us in the proposed conference.

[8, pp. 107–109] II: 264.

Sandino's Protocol for Peace

(Instructions for peace negotiations given to Sofonías Salvatierra, January 20, 1933)

First: Know precisely the political program that Dr. Sacasa will develop during his four-year administration. Be certain

---

(July 14–16, 1932) Fighting continues in Jinotega and León. (September 13, 1932) Admiral Woodward secretly orders U.S. warships to stand off the Nicaraguan coasts. (October 2, 1932) Sandino's Eighth Column attacks San Francisco del Carnicero on north shore of Lake Managua. *(October 3, 1932) Nicaraguan Liberal and Conservative parties join in signing a "patriotic pact" to deal with Sandino. (October 28, 1932) The U.S. ambassador announces support for Anastasio Somoza García to direct the Nicaraguan National Guard.*

that he will absolutely get rid of foreign intervention in Nicaraguan finances; what he intends to do with regard to the so-called National Guard; and, whether Dr. Sacasa has agreements of any kind signed with the North Americans.

Second: Propose that, by initiative of the Executive, the National Nicaraguan Congress decree the creation of a new province in uncultivated national lands between the zones of El Chipote and the Atlantic Coast, with the name of "Luz y Verdad". . . . This does not in any way imply a reward to our Army, much less to me. The purpose is to enhance the Homeland in general.

Third: Propose that by initiative of the Executive, a decree be issued to maintain in the Province Luz y Verdad all the war equipment used during the war of National Honor. . . .

Fourth: Propose a decree by the National Congress to extract from the national ar-

chives and burn all the documents that qualify as "banditry" the patriotic attitude of our Army. . . . This is a question of national dignity. It was because of this attitude that Nicaragua continues to be free, sovereign, and independent.

Fifth: The Army Defending the National Sovereignty of Nicaragua asks for the revision of the Bryan-Chamorro treaties . . . imposed by the intervention of North America. Furthermore, the Army demands that the Canal Route through Nicaragua and the possible construction of a Naval Base in the Gulf of Fonseca be declared as belonging to the Indio-Hispanic Nationality.

[8, pp. 135–138] II: 269–271.

(November 6, 1932) Juan B. Sacasa elected president. The United States expresses its support. (December 24, 1932) Sandino announces he is ready to join in a search for peace and names his delegation. (December 26, 1932) Gen. Juan P. Umanzor's column attacks the railroad at El Sauce.

Uneasy Victory

January 1933 to mid-February 1934

Violations Continue Despite Cease-Fire

(Letter to Sofonías Salvatierra, January 25, 1933)

My wife informs me that she understood from you and señor Sacasa that orders were drawn up against attacking our positions. However, we are sad to tell you that our cavalry commanded by General Gómez was attacked in Las Minitas on the 22nd, and again on the 24th in Saraguazca. . . .

By the way, I take this opportunity to declare to the people of Nicaragua that we are not an obstacle to peace. We are enemies of war. We have only been exercising our rights of defense. My telegram indicated that we have ordered our forces to suspend hostilities.

Patria y Libertad.

[8, pp. 161–162] II: 272.

Sandino Goes to Attempt Peace Accord with President Sacasa

(Discourse to troops, February 2, 1933)

Brothers:

We have fought to keep our country free from foreign interventionists. The yankee has left, but, artfully, he thinks that he will come back soon on the hope that we will continue to fight. But he is wrong. I think that peace should be made within these next five days, and to achieve this I believe that the best thing is for me to go reach an understanding with Dr. Sacasa. In my place I leave General Lara for the days I am absent.

If Doctor Sacasa is disposed to take me prisoner instead of hearing us, I will kill myself, and if I don't do it, each one of you is authorized to spit in my face as a traitor.

[8, pp. 179–180] II: 277.

Provisions to Disband Sandino's Army after Peace Accord

(Circular to all the Commanders, February 4, 1933)

Dear brothers:

After having left the peace of Nicaragua satisfactorily and completely arranged, I returned yesterday to this Provisional General Headquarters of our Army. Would you, upon receiving this circular, regroup immediately with all the war equipment under your custody to the town of San Rafael del Norte, where I will be with the rest of the forces from the 6th of this month forward. There you will receive my personal instructions regarding all the arrangements just made, including guarantees for your security. Besides, there are no longer any differences between the armies in Nicaragua, because we are united sincerely and really with Dr. Sacasa. Our word to him will influ-

---

(January 1, 1933) United States Marines are recalled from Nicaragua, President Juan B. Sacasa is inaugurated, and Anastasio Somoza García assumes directorship of the National Guard. *(January 6, 1933)* Sandino announces his terms for peace. *(January 19, 1933)* Sacasa's peace dele- gation arrives in Sandino's camp and Sandino presents his "Protocol for Peace." *(January 23, 1933)* A truce is declared. *(January 25, 1933)* The National Guard attacks Sandinistas in Saraguazca.

ence the satisfactory resolution of any remaining issues.

[11, p. 458] II: 284.

Sandino's Economic Vision for Nicaragua

(*Interview with Ramón Belausteguigoitia, Spanish journalist, February 1933*)

"Do you believe in the development of capital?"

—Without doubt capital can do its work and develop, but the worker must not be humiliated and exploited.

"Do you have the ambition of possessing your own land?"

—Ah! They believe out there that I am going to convert myself into a large landholder! No, nothing of this. I will never have properties.

"Do you believe in the transformation of societies by pressure of the State, or by the reform of individuals?"

—By internal reform. State pressure changes the exterior, the apparent. We think that every man should be a brother, not a wolf. The rest is mechanical, external, superficial. Naturally the State has to intervene.

[3, chapters XII, XIII, and XIV] II: 294–295, 298.

Sandino Defends His Right to Make Peace

(*March 16, 1933*)

Señor Gustavo Alemán Bolaños, Guatemala City

Concerning your opinion of the peace treaty signed on February 2nd, I say that you are unjust and make yourself a moral assassin, because you kill the vision I have of the restoration of our national autonomy.

I have not been the victim of anyone's suggestion. I am the only one to blame for the good or the evil of this treaty. . . .

Permit me to remind you that in the seven years of war we never received one little bullet and we have defended ourselves "with the pure heart of Jesus." You have no right to demand Nicaraguan independence with one quick blow. Regarding whether I have fallen from a pedestal, of which I am unaware, to reduce myself to a little boy, I agree. After all, I am not even a military man and nothing more than a peasant fighting for the autonomy of our country.

[1, pp. 160–161] II: 330–331.

Sandino Makes Provisions for His Men and Awaits the Birth of a Son

(*Circular to his lieutenants, May 2, 1933*)

Notwithstanding our enemies that still

(February 2, 1933) Sandino flies to Managua to sign the peace treaty, and is acclaimed by crowds in the capital streets. He signs a peace agreement at the presidential palace at midnight. *(February 9, 1933) Amnesty is declared for all Sandinista combatants.* *(February 22, 1933) The Army* *Defending the National Sovereignty of Nicaragua is demobilized at San Rafael del Norte.* *(May 1933) Sandino and his men establish an agricultural cooperative in Wiwilí on the Río Coco, Segovias.*

surround Dr. Sacasa, he received our Commission well and agreed to pay eleven hundred and some pesos monthly for the one hundred men [Emergency Guard]. The government will also provide a hundred uniforms for the men. . . . Naturally the food will be paid for each lad, since the ten pesos will not stretch enough to sustain a family.

. . . . The Government has provided us with a quantity of provisions, machetes, and other implements, so that we can establish a commissary so the hundred men and others who dedicate themselves to cultivation and to panning for gold can buy food. . . .

During these days I remain in San Rafael del Norte waiting to give a happy welcome to a son. I may take a short trip to Managua to put things on a more solid basis for the common good.

Patria y Libertad.

[11, pp. 440–442] II: 332–334.

Before the Coffin of His Wife

(June 2, 1933)

My dear brothers, to this good woman whom now we bury, to her great spirit of love and of goodness, all of us owe the peace of Nicaragua. Perhaps people will criticize me because her coffin is white, but martyrs as well as angels have the right to come in white to the grave. And this woman is a martyr of Nicaragua.

Because of Blanca, neither the bandits who once detained me in Jinotega nor the yankee invaders are kicking us around any longer.

It is better that I keep quiet because I am getting irritated.

[14, Año IV, No. 1082, June 2, 1933, p. 2] II: 339.

A New Social Order for the Poor

Wiwilí, Río Coco, Nicaragua, C. A.
July 16, 1933

Rafael Ramírez Delgado,
Honduras

Very esteemed sir:

In this river port from where I write you, it gives me satisfaction to put ourselves at your orders. Here I am dedicated to founding a society of mutual help and universal brotherhood. I want to do my little bit in favor of the emancipation and welfare of the working class, which, as you know, has always been exploited and looked down upon by the bureaucratic bourgeoisie. This is the problem that many men of philosophy and love try to resolve. Now that the Excellent Mr. President of the Republic gives me protection through the Peace Treaty, I want to make of these virgin and exuberant regions a place of life and a center of civilization for

(May 20, 1933) Sandino travels a second time to Managua at President Sacasa's invitation for discussions. He meets with workers, students, and professionals to form the Autonomist Party. (June 2, 1933) Sandino's wife Blanca Aráuz dies giving birth to a daughter, Blanca Segovia Sandino. (August 20, 1933) A patrol of the National Guard attacks the Sandinistas near Yalí. (November 20, 1933) Sandino travels to Managua a third time to discuss with Sacasa the growing conflicts with the National Guard in the northern provinces.

all the families that are at risk in the heart of the octopus-cities, disinherited and scourged by misery.

[2, p. 67] II: 343–344.

New Level of Dangers to Sandino

(Related to Nicolás Arrieta, November 1933)

"Do you not fear, General, that something will happen to you?"

No, not at all. I trust Sacasa. I believe in him. I am certain of his sincerity. Several friends have warned me that I run risks, but I do not believe Salvatierra would play a dirty trick on me. After all, I exposed myself to a thousand dangers in the mountains for the cause of the Homeland. Why not continue confronting dangers for this cause?

Before coming here, I reflected on whether it was an ambush; nevertheless, I considered it my duty to come to continue the struggle on behalf of the Nicaraguan people.

[17, 21 p.] II: 360.

Reflections on Decapitation of the Enemy

(Conversation with Nicolás Arrieta in Niquinohomo, November 1933)

"What of the decapitation of which so much has been said?"

To cut off a man's head is a terrible thing. But these dogs obligated us to this type of fight. They arrived at peasants' huts, tied the whole family up, and set fire to them. Many, with their relatives, saw these atrocities from a distance and came to join our ranks.

They also killed our people and cut off their heads and stuck them on trees along the roads. We had to give satisfaction to our people and to the outraged peasants. Nevertheless, we set the national soldiers free.

[17, 21 pp.] II: 361–362.

Sandino Visits His Natural Mother

(Conversation with Nicolás Arrieta in Niquinohomo, November 1933)

I just went to visit my mother. When I entered she didn't recognize me since it had been years.

I said: "I am Augusto César." She told me that she had heard that I was around here.

She had other children and she lives poor. She asked me to buy her a little house. I am going to buy it for her.

Just as does every poor person in Nicaragua, she also wants a little house. We will not permit that another Nicaraguan lack his own house.

[17, 21 p.] II: 365.

(November 28, 1933) Arthur Bliss Lane arrives in Nicaragua as U.S. Ambassador. (January 26, 1934) Sandino writes to President Sacasa pointing out the unconstitutionality of the National Guard. (February 16, 1934) At Sacasa's invitation, Sandino arrives in Managua for "frank discussions," accompanied by his brother Sócrates and Generals Estrada and Umanzor.

The Final Days

SANDINO IS BETRAYED

February 17–21, 1934

Sandino Resists Attempts by All Ideologies to Distort the Resistance

(Conversation with journalist Ramón Belausteguigoitia, February 1933)

"It has been said that your rebellion has a marked social character. It has even been labeled as communist. . . . Is there a social program?"

On different occasions there have been attempts to distort this movement of national defense, converting it into a social struggle. I have opposed this with all my strength. This movement is nationalist and anti-imperialist. We maintain aloft the flag of liberty for Nicaragua and for all Hispano-America. As for the rest, the social grounds, this movement is popular and we recognize a sense of advance in social aspirations. Representatives from the International Federation of Labor, the Anti-Imperialist League, the Quakers,

(February 17, 1934) Sandino publicly declares the National Guard unconstitutional. *(February 18, 1934)* La Prensa *calls for Sandino to turn over the rest of his arms. Sandino meets with Sacasa and Somoza at the presidential house.*

have come here to see us, to influence us. . . . [Farabundo] Martí, propagandist of communism, saw that he could not achieve his program and he left [for El Salvador].

[3, Chapters XII, XIII, and XIV] II: 293.

Sandino Plans to Retire to the Cooperative on the Río Coco

(Conversation with Nicolás Arrieta in Niquinohomo, November 1933)

"And you do not aspire to the presidency, General?"

No, not one moment. What I want is to go work hard in the mountains, to serve the thousands and thousands of peasants who have supported our struggle. . . . We are going to cut down trees in the mountains and make an agricultural co-operative, where we will all be brothers.

(February 20, 1934) Sacasa names Sandinista General Portocarrero as Presidential Delegate to the northern region, against Somoza's open objection.

These peasant farmers are great workers. We are going to erect schools, construct cities. We will bring carpenters from the Pacific, mechanics, leather-workers, tailors, so that we can have it all. That's right, there will be no vagrant drunkards, egoists, exploiters. All will be in cooperatives. There is gold in abundance and with it we will buy all we need. The timber is magnificent to build houses and furniture with. Now the peasants don't have anything, but they will have it all.

[17, 21 pp.] II: 364.

Wiwilí Cooperative Surrounded by Somoza's National Guard

(Conversation with Sofonías Salvatierra, February 15–16, 1934)

They are surrounding me. For about a month the Guard has been taking positions around Wiwilí. What is this? The President is fooling me. ("No, the President is loyal," objected Salvatierra.) Well, then, his subordinates do what they wish. The guards say they are going to destroy me. Destroy—destroy—as if we don't know what we have to do. Destroy men who live working and teaching the nation how to work. The Guardsmen are a burden to the public Treasury, improvised little officials who have nothing else to do but eat and drink.

General Somoza thinks to destroy me. And what good is General Somoza? He is useful for a job. Afterwards, no one will see him again. . . .

I do not want war, but how is it possible that my people cannot live in peace on their own land. The Guard is killing them. Every day they kill them.

[8, pp. 233–234; 237–238] II: 373–374.

Illegal National Guard Threatens Stability

("Report" in La Prensa, *February 18, 1934)*

I will not surrender my weapons to the National Guard, because it is not a duly constituted authority. They have killed seventeen of my companions and the Segovian jails are full of Sandinistas. I do not want war, preferring to abandon the country, but I will not influence my men to do the same.

"But the National Guard has left you tranquil in Wiwilí."

They have not let us work freely. They persecute the Sandinistas that come to our camps looking for work. They have not come to Wiwilí, naturally, because we are armed.

"General, don't you think the Guard is obliged to see that there are not two states within one?"

(February 21, 1934) After a telephone conversation, Ambassador Arthur Bliss Lane and Anastasio Somoza García meet. Later, Lane meets Moncada for lunch. At six in the evening, Somoza meets with sixteen of his Guardsmen. In the evening, Sandino dines with President Sacasa in the presidential house. Sandino leaves in a car with his father, minister Salvatierra, and Generals Francisco Estrada and Pablo Umanzor. The car is detained by a National Guard patrol at the Campo de Marte quarters. Gregorio Sandino and Salvatierra are detained and the others taken. Augusto Sandino is

When the situation in the country is normalized, yes, sir. But the fact is that here there are not two states, but three: the President's forces, that of the National Guard, and mine. The Guard does not obey the President; we do not obey the Guard, because it is illegal, and so it goes.

"It is said that the National Guard is elaborating a project to reform its regulations to be adapted to the laws of the country, properly approved by Congress. What do you say to this?"

Well this is very wise. This is the route that ought to be taken. Give it legal form and then we can believe that they will not harass us.

"The public is concerned about these matters and at times it is thought that this could result in another internal conflict."

I do not want war, nothing will bring me to it again. I repeat that I will leave the country before bloodying it and bathing many homes with tears. My forces have

backed the President. This has been my purpose, and with much pleasure I will dedicate myself to cultivating the earth. I will pay taxes to sustain the State as long as the Guard is included within the framework of the law.

[15, February 18, 1934] II: 375–379.

Appeal to President Sacasa to Reorganize the National Guard to Guarantee Safety

Managua, D. N. 19th of February, 1934

Most excellent Sr. President of the Republic, Doctor Juan B. Sacasa Presidential Palace

I understand your fervent desires to channel the country within our laws, but there is the inconsistency of two armies, that is, the National Guard with unconstitutional procedures, and your Protective Guard of Emergency on the Río Coco under the

command of Generals Francisco Estrada and Juan Santos Morales. The latter force was constitutional from the moment you, as President, established it, and it is up to you whether it continues or not.

Nevertheless, Mr. President, the Treaty effectively guarantees the lives and interests of all the men who fought under my orders in the recent campaigns. . . . This indispensable guarantee cannot be effected without correcting the illegal form and procedures of the National Guard.

[8, pp. 239–242] II: 379–380.

---

executed, along with his faithful generals. Sócrates Sandino had suffered the same fate a few minutes before. **(February 1934)** *Sacasa condemns the murders and orders an investigation. Nothing is determined. In diverse parts of the world, there are demonstrations repudiating the crime.*

(March 3, 1934) *The National Guard attacks the Wiwilí cooperative, killing many. Sandinista General Abraham Rivera surrenders.*

Growing Premonition of Assassination

February 1, 1933

Final orders to brother General Escolástico Lara as Interim Supreme Commander of our Army:

If the fifth of this month passes and there is no notice of me, it is a sure sign that I am dead. Then all the armed forces concentrated here will proceed to take the course that they desire with the commander that each soldier chooses.

General Lara is free to continue the revolution or to retire to his native town.

Provisional General Headquarters.

Patria y Libertad.

A. C. Sandino

[11, pp. 444–445] II: 276.

Others Will Continue the Struggle for National Sovereignty

Each abuse of power hastens the destruction of him who exercises it. We will go toward the sun of liberty or toward death. And if we die, our cause will continue to live. Others will follow us.

[13, Año II, No. 571, 1928, p. 17] I: 241.

(Told to Enrique Sánchez as recounted by Gustavo Bolaños, circa 1934)

I will not live a long time. But here are the lads who will continue the struggle that we embarked upon. They will be able to achieve great things. . . .

[1, pp. 112–113] II: 381.

(June 3, 1934) Anastasio Somoza García accepts responsibility for Sandino's assassination. *(August 25, 1934)* The Nicaraguan National Congress decrees amnesty for all who had committed any crime from February 16, 1933 to this date, thus exonerating Anastasio Somoza.

Documentary Sources

The citations in brackets following the documents in the text are keyed by number to the sources listed below. Nonbracketed references in the text refer to volume and page(s) in Sergio Ramírez, *Augusto C. Sandino: El pensamiento vivo*, Editorial Nueva Nicaragua, 1981.

Books

1   Alemán Bolaños, Gustavo, *Sandino, el libertador*. México/Guatemala, Ediciones Caribe, 1951, 248 p.

2   Arellano, Jorge Eduardo, *Augusto César Sandino. Escritos literarios y documentos desconocidos*. Managua, Ministerio de Cultura, 1980, 98 p.

3   Belausteguigoitia, Ramón de, *Con*

Sandino en Nicaragua. Managua, Nueva Nicaragua, 1981, 244 p.

4 Calderón Ramírez, Salvador, *Los últimos días de Sandino.* México, D.F., Ediciones Botas, 1934, 164 p.

5 Campos Ponce, Xavier, *Los yankis y Sandino.* México, D.F., 1962, 278 p.

6 Maraboto, Emigdio, *Sandino ante el coloso.* Veracruz, México, Ed. L & M., S. en C., 1929, 36 p.

7 Román, José, *Maldito país.* (s.c.), inédito, 1933, 173 folios.

8 Salvatierra, Sofonías, *Sandino o la tragedia de un pueblo.* Madrid, España, 1934, 291 p.

9 Selser, Gregorio, *Sandino, general de hombres libres.* Buenos Aires, Argentina, Editorial Triángulo, 1958, Tomo I, 375 p.

10 Selser, Gregorio, *op. cit.,* Tomo II, 399 p.

11 Somoza García, Anastasio, *El verdadero Sandino o el calvario de las Segovias.* Managua, Nicaragua, Tipografía Robelo, 1936, 566 p.

Periodicals

12 Ariel. Tegucigalpa, Honduras. Revista quincenal fundada por el poeta y periodista hondureño Froylán Turcios, entre 1924 y 1925.

13 El Universal Gráfico. México, D.F. Suplemento semanal del diario *El Universal.*

14 El Nuevo Diario. Managua, Nicaragua. Diario fundado en 1980.

15 La Prensa. Managua, Nicaragua. Diario fundado en 1926.

Archives

16 Archivo del Instituto de Estudio del Sandinismo; fondo Pedro José Zepeda.

17 Archivo del Instituto de Estudio del Sandinismo; fondo general.

Photo on page i from *El verdadero Sandino o el calvario de las Segovias,* by Anastasio Somoza García (Managua: Tipografia Robelo, 1936), p. 325.

EDITOR: NANCY ANN MILLER
BOOK DESIGNER: SHARON L. SKLAR
JACKET DESIGNER: SHARON L. SKLAR
PRODUCTION COORDINATOR: HARRIET CURRY
TYPEFACE: PALATINO
TYPESETTER: G&S TYPESETTERS
PRINTER/BINDER: EVERBEST PRINTING CO., LTD.